Modern Poetry in Trans

Series Three, Number 9

CH00967740

Palestine

Edited by David and Helen Constantine

MODERN POETRY IN TRANSLATION

Modern Poetry in Translation
Series Three, No. 9
© Modern Poetry in Translation 2008 and contributors
ISBN 978-0-954536-79-4

Printed and bound in Great Britain by Short Run Press, Exeter

Editors: David and Helen Constantine
Reviews Editor: Josephine Balmer
Administrators: Deborah de Kock and Angela Holton

Submissions should be sent in hard copy, with return postage, to David
and Helen Constantine, *Modern Poetry in Translation*, The Queen's College,
Oxford, OX1 4AW. Unless agreed in advance, submissions by email will
not be accepted. Only very exceptionally will we consider work that has
already been published elsewhere. Translators are themselves responsible
for obtaining any necessary permissions. Since we do sometimes authorize
further publication on one or two very reputable websites of work that has
appeared in *MPT*, the permissions should cover that possibility.

Founding Editors: Ted Hughes and Daniel Weissbort

Subscription Rates: (including postage)

	UK	Overseas
Single Issue	£11	£13 / US$ 26
One year subscription (2 issues, surface mail)	£22	£26 / US$ 52
Two year subscription (4 issues, surface mail)	£40	£48 / US$ 96

To subscribe please use the subscription form at the back of the magazine.
Discounts available.

To pay by credit card please visit www.mptmagazine.com

Modern Poetry in Translation is represented in the UK by
Inpress Limted – www.inpressbooks.co.uk
and distributed by Central Books, 99 Wallis Road, London, E9 5LN,
www.centralbooks.com

For orders: tel +44 (0) 845 458 9911 Fax +44 (0) 845 458 9912
or visit www.mptmagazine.com

Modern Poetry in Translation Limited. A Company Limited by Guarantee.
Registered in England and Wales, Number 5881603.
UK Registered Charity Number 1118223.

Contents

Reviews

Instead of an editorial
Seventeen notes and quotations having to do with Palestine

---

1. Something there is that doesn't love a wall. (Robert Frost)

2. The potency of the idea of the vendetta was clearly demonstrated in the opening act of the crusade, the 'first holocaust' of European Jews. The first acts of violent anti-semitism seem to have occurred in France shortly after the Council of Clermont [November 1095]. They then spread to Germany and eastern Europe, where they were associated with the first waves of crusaders leaving for the East in the spring of 1096. On 3 May the storm broke over the Jewish community at Speyer, where a south German army under Emich of Leiningen, the most merciless of the persecutors, had gathered. Emich proceeded to Worms, where the massacres began on 18 May, and then to Mainz, where he was joined by more Germans and by a large army of French, English, Flemish and Lorrainer crusaders. Between 25 and 29 May the Jewish community at Mainz, one of the largest in Europe, was decimated. Some crusaders then marched north to Cologne, from where the Jews had already been dispersed into neighbouring settlements. For the next month they were hunted out and destroyed. Another band seems to have gone south-west to Trier and Metz, where the massacres

continued. Meanwhile another crusading army, probably Peter the Hermit's, forced almost the whole community at Regensburg to undergo baptism and the communities at Wesseli and Prague in Bohemia suffered probably from the attentions of yet another crusading army, led by a priest called Folkmar.

These pogroms were attributed by some contemporaries to avarice, and the crusaders certainly made financial demands of the Jewish communities and despoiled them; indeed, given the demands of the journey they were about to make they were obviously obsessed with cash. But the Hebrew accounts ascribed greed more to local bishops, their officials and townspeople than to the crusaders, who seem to have been more interested in forcing conversions. Everywhere Jews were offered the choice of conversion or death, and synagogues, Torah scrolls and cemeteries were desecrated. The Jews feared that the crusaders intended to wipe Judaism out of the regions through which they passed. There is overwhelming evidence that uppermost in the crusaders' minds was a desire for vengeance. They found it impossible to distinguish between Muslims and Jews and if they were being called upon, as they saw it, to avenge the injury to Christ's 'honour' of the loss of his patrimony to the Muslims [their occupation of Jerusalem in 638], why, they asked, should they not also avenge the injury to his person of the Crucifixion – a far deeper disparagement of his 'honour' – particularly in the light of a popular legend circulating at the time in which Christ on the cross had called on the faithful to avenge him? [. . .] Throughout the twelfth century every major call to crusade gave rise to pogroms against Jews.

                                  (Jonathan Riley-Smith, *The Crusades*)

3.   There is a green hill far away,
         Without a city wall,
      Where the dear Lord was crucified,
         Who died to save us all.

4. At the very centre of the Hereford *Mappa Mundi* (c. 1300) is Calvary.

> This was a pleasant place
> This was a green hill outside the city.
> Who would believe it now? Unthink
> The blood if you can, the pocks, the scabs,
> The tendrils of wire. Imagine an apple tree
> Where that thing stands embedded.

5. *Father Zosimus crosses the Jordan and enters the desert. There he finds Mary the Egyptian entirely naked and burned black by the sun. She begs him to lend her his cloak, to cover herself. Then she tells him her story:*

I was born in Egypt and at the age of twelve I went to Alexandria and there for seventeen years I gave myself over to public depravity. I never said no to any man. And when the men of that country were preparing to make the voyage to Jerusalem to adore the True Cross I begged the sailors who were conveying them to let me go too. When they asked me for the fare I answered, 'Brothers, I have nothing to give you, but take my body as payment for the voyage'. On those terms they took me and used my body as their payment. We arrived together in Jerusalem and presenting myself with the others at the doors of the church to adore the True Cross I was suddenly repulsed by an invisible force. Several times I returned to the doors of the church, but in vain: each time I felt myself prevented while the others entered without difficulty. Thereupon I entered into myself and reflected that my numerous and filthy sins were the cause of my being repulsed. I began to sigh deeply, to shed bitter tears and to chastise my body with my hands. Examining the church door, I saw an image of the Blessed Virgin Mary and at once I began praying to her very humbly that she would forgive my sins and let me enter to adore the Holy Cross. And I promised her I would renounce the world and in future take a vow of chastity. Then I put my trust in the Blessed Virgin and this time entered

the church without hindrance. After I had with great devotion
adored the Holy Cross a man gave me three pennies with which
I bought three loaves. And then I heard a voice saying to me, 'If
you cross the Jordan you will be saved'. So I crossed the Jordan
and came into this desert where I have been for forty-seven
years without seeing a man. The three loaves I brought with me
hardened and have lasted me till now. My clothes went to rags
and for the first seventeen years of my solitary life I suffered
the temptations of the flesh but through the grace of God I
conquered them all. Now I have told you my story and I ask you
to pray to God for me.

(Jacques de Voragine, *La Légende dorée*)

6.   O little town of Bethlehem,
          How still we see thee lie!
      Above thy deep and dreamless sleep
          The silent stars go by.
      Yet in thy dark street shineth
          The everlasting light;
      The hopes and fears of all the years
          Are met in thee tonight.

7. Nothing is more difficult than to determine what a child
takes in, and does not take in, of its environment and its teaching.
This fact is brought home to me by the hymns which I learned
as a child, and never forgot. They mean to me almost more than
the finest poetry, and they have for me a more permanent value,
somehow or other...

      Each gentle dove
      And sighing bough
      That makes the eve
      So fair to me
      Has something far
      Diviner now
      To draw me back

To Galilee.
O Galilee, sweet Galilee
Where Jesus loved so much to be,
O Galilee, sweet Galilee,
Come sing thy songs again to me!

To me the word Galilee has a wonderful sound. The lake of
Galilee! I don't want to know where it is. I never want to go to
Palestine. Galilee is one of those lovely, glamorous words, not
places, that exist in the golden haze of a child's half-formed
imagination. And in my man's imagination it is just the same.
It has been left untouched. With regard to the hymns that had
such a profound influence on my childish consciousness, there
has been no crystallizing out, no dwindling into actuality, no
hardening into commonplace. They are the same to my man's
experience as they were to me nearly forty years ago . . .

Sun of my soul, thou Saviour dear,
It is not night if Thou be near . . .

That was the last hymn at the board-school. It did not mean to
me any Christian dogma or any salvation. Just the words, 'Sun of
my soul, thou Saviour dear', penetrated me with wonder and the
mystery of twilight. At another time the last hymn was:

Fair waved the golden corn
In Canaan's pleasant land . . .

And again I loved 'Canaan's pleasant land.' The wonder of
'Canaan', which could never be localized.
    I think it was good to be brought up a Protestant: and among
Protestants, a Nonconformist, and among Nonconformists, a
Congregationalist. Which sounds pharisaic. But I should have
missed bitterly a direct knowledge of the Bible, and a direct
relation to Galilee and Canaan, Moab and Kedron, those places
that never existed on earth. And in the Church of England one

would hardly have escaped those snobbish hierarchies of class, which spoil so much for a child. And the Primitive Methodists, when I was a boy, were always having 'revivals' and being 'saved', and I always had a horror of being saved.

(D.H.Lawrence, 'Hymns in a Man's Life')

8. The northwest town of Qalqilya (population 50,000) is totally surrounded by seventeen kilometres of the wall, with only one exit. The once bustling main street now ends in the wall's waste land. The town's meagre economy is consequently in ruins. A market gardener trundles a wheelbarrow of sand to distribute round some plants before the coming winter. Until the wall he employed twelve workers. (95% of Palestinian businesses have fewer than five employees.) Today he employs nobody. The sales of his plants – because the town has been cut off – have been reduced by 90%. He throws away instead of collecting the seeds from a heap of flowers. His large hands are heavy with the admission that henceforth here they have nothing to do.

Difficult to convey the sight of the wall where it crosses the land where there is nobody. It's the opposite of rubble. It is bureaucratic – carefully planned on electronic maps, prefabricated and pre-emptive. Its purpose is to prevent the creation of a Palestinian state. The aim of the sledgehammer. Since it began to be built three years ago, there has been no significant reduction in the number of kamikaze attacks. Standing before it, you feel as short as a cigarette butt. (Except during Ramadan, most Palestinians smoke a lot.) Yet, oddly, it doesn't look final, only insurmountable.

When it's finished, it will be the 640-km-long expressionless face of an inequality. At the moment it's 210 km long. The inequality is between those who have the full arsenal of the latest military technology to defend what they believe to be their interest (Apache helicopters, Merkava tanks, F16's) and those who have nothing, save their names and a shared belief that justice is axiomatic. The stance of undefeated despair works like this.

It could be that the wall belongs to the same shortsighted repressive logic as the 'sonic boom' bombing that the inhabitants of Gaza are being submitted to every night as I write. Jet fighters dive very low at full speed to break the sound barrier, and the nerves of those huddling sleepless below with their axiom. And it won't work.

Such a superiority of firepower discourages intelligent strategy; to think strategically one has to be able to imagine oneself in one's opponent's place, and a habitual sense of superiority precludes this.

Climb one of the jabals and look down at the wall, way below, winding its geometric dividers' course towards the southern horizon. Did you see the hoopoe bird? In the long-term view the wall looks make-shift.

(John Berger, 'Undefeated Despair', 2005)

9.   And did those feet in ancient time
      Walk upon England's mountains green?
      And was the holy Lamb of God
      On England's pleasant pastures seen?

      And did the Countenance Divine
      Shine forth upon our clouded hills
      And was Jerusalem builded here
      Among those dark Satanic mills?

Blake wanted a New Jerusalem in which relations between men and women would not be spoiled by priests and there would be no more such injustice as he condemned in 'Holy Thursday'. His Christ was a radical opponent of the old corrupt order of Church and Kings. And at the root of his famous battle hymn of the New Republic there may well be the encouraging legend that Christ as a child once came from Nazareth to England in the company of Joseph of Arimathea – the same Joseph who returned perhaps half a century later, over the flooded Somerset levels, by boat to Glastonbury, the Isle of Avalon, with Christ's blood in the Grail. Once the Word had gone out, through the diaspora of the Apostles and through the translations done by Jerome (who settled in Bethlehem), countries far from Palestine wanted connection with that land. So the Three Marys landed in the Camargue, for example. And at Blake's turn of the century, which was the age of Tom Paine's *Rights of Man* and Mary Wollstonecraft's *Rights Of Woman*, there blew into an England, then, as now, desperately in need of it, the new testament of liberty, equality and fraternity.

10.   On the wall was written in chalk
      They want a war.
      The man who wrote it
      Is already dead.   (Brecht)

11. Paradise has, so to speak, been dispersed all over the earth and is for that reason no longer recognizable – Its scattered features want reuniting – its skeleton wants filling out again. The regeneration of Paradise. (Novalis)

12. During the nineteenth century fragments of Palestine, in the form of place-names, were scattered through Britain, sparsely in some regions, densely in others, by the builders of non-conformist chapels. They shine on maps, as they do in the verses of hymns, with a strange beauty and poignancy, for the hope and aspiration they represent.

Some have to do with water: Rehoboth, where Isaac dug a new well that no one would dispute or seek to rob him of; Siloam, where Christ gave sight to the man born blind (he spat in the dirt, rubbed the wet dirt in the blind man's eyes and said, 'Go wash in the pool of Siloam'); Bethesda, the pool, where 'lay a great multitude of impotent folk, of blind, halt, withered, waiting for the moving of the water', where Christ healed the man who could never get into the pool when the angel came; and Bethania, which may be 'Bethabara beyond Jordan where John was baptizing', or, more likely, Bethany, the home village of Mary,

Martha and their brother Lazarus, the leper, whom Christ fetched back from the dead. These potent places! Transplanted into the locations of ordinary hardworking lives. Others have to do with vision and promise, they are the hills and mountains: Horeb, where God spoke to Moses out of the Burning Bush; Nebo, from where you could see the Promised Land; Hermon, where Christ was transfigured. Such naming must raise aspirations very high indeed. Carmel, for its fertility; Sharon for its legendary beauty; Beulah, a name that means marriage, so the wedding of people to a beloved native land. And Salem – the word means peace – taken by most commentators to mean Jerusalem itself, the New Jerusalem of peace and justice, built by believing men and women in a promising homeland.

There are clusters of such names on the slate in Gwynedd: Carmel and Bethlehem by Bethesda; Carmel, Nebo and Nasareth in among the quarries of Nantlle. The workings are long since finished, the wreckage remains, as do the slate graveyards and in them the quarrymen dead of the dust. The light glints off the slate heaps as it does off a crow's wings. Any footstep on them sounds with a clatter. But there is always a trickle, a whispering or a din of the surviving streams. Of the chapels themselves, giant survivals, too big for what community is left, many have gone to ruin or have been put to such modern uses as selling antiques. But I know of at least one Bethel – the name means house of God – with a smokey flue and flaking plaster where they act the Nativity every year with believing children and a real lamb. What miracles the choirs in unison sang for in their heyday! For health, prosperity, peace, the keeping of promises.

13. Palestinians now make up approximately 22% of the population of Israel. This is a larger percentage than was ever represented by a Jewish minority in any country in any period of history. The total number of Palestinians living within Israel and the occupied territories (that is, greater Israel for the Israelis or greater Palestine for the Palestinians) is already larger

than the Jewish population [. . .] Israelis and Palestinians alike
should join me in taking dual citizenship – for we share one
destiny.

(Daniel Barenboim)

14. The Emperor Constantine, become a Christian, sent his
mother Helena to Jerusalem, to find the True Cross. Arriving
in Jerusalem, she summoned all the Rabbis of Palestine. They
were very alarmed. They guessed she wanted the Cross, whose
whereabouts they had sworn never to reveal, not even under
torture, since its discovery would mean the end of the Jews'
supremacy in Palestine. She asked, they refused to tell her, she
ordered them all to be burned. This moved them. They delivered
up to her a man called Judas (not Iscariot), saying that he might
tell. She gave him a choice: tell me or die of starvation. Rather
die, he said. But after six days going hungry, he relented, and
led her to the place, on which stood a temple of Venus. Helena
prayed, there came an earthquake and such a heavenly perfume
that Judas was converted. Helena cleared the site of Venus'
temple and ordered Judas to dig. Twenty feet down he found
three crosses. The True Cross was soon identified, for by its
power a woman was restored to health or, some say, a man to life.
Judas was baptized and became Bishop Cyriacus. Then Helena
sent him to find the nails of the Cross. He did, they shone like
gold. Saint Helena took them home to her son, who wore them
on his helmet and bridle.

In Wales this Helena, the daughter of an English publican,
has been confused with Elen of Caernarfon, a more attractive
personage. She was the daughter of Eudwy, a Welsh chieftain
who lived near the Roman fort of Segontium. She married
Macsen who, as Magnus Clemens Maximus, was emperor in
Britain, Gaul and Spain, and by him she had a boy called
Constantine. Her story is told in the *Mabinogion*, in 'The Dream
of Macsen Wledig'. She was a magical builder of roads, the great
Sarn Helen, which runs from Segontium (now Caernarfon) south
through the length of Wales, being the best known of them. She

is the patron saint of roadbuilders and a protector of travellers. And by confusion a traveller to Palestine and Inventor of the True Cross.

15. How are we doing? Glance at the FTSE. And what about the Rapture Index? 18 February 2008 it stands at 166. Good or bad? Depends on your point of view. But we should understand what the Rapture Index is.

> The Rapture Index has two functions: one is to factor together a number of related end-time components into a cohesive indicator, and the other is to standardize those components to eliminate the wide variance that currently exists with prophecy reporting. The Rapture Index is by no means intended to predict the Rapture. However, the index is designed to measure the type of activity that could act as a precursor to the Rapture. You could say the Rapture index is a Dow Jones Industrial Average of end-time activity, but you might do better to view it as a prophetic speedometer. The higher the number, the faster we're moving towards the Rapture.
> **Rapture Index of 100 and below: Slow prophetic activity**
> **Rapture Index of 100 to 130: Moderate prophetic activity**
> **Rapture Index of 130 to 160: Heavy prophetic activity**
> **Rapture Index above 160: Fasten your seat belts**

When calculating the Rapture Index forty-five variables have to be factored in, among them Leadership, Volcanoes, False Christs, Liberalism, Food Supply, Beast Government, Gog (Russia), Inflation, Drug Abuse, Satanism and the Peace Process. Not everyone wants peace in Palestine. Some want Armageddon. Come Armageddon, come the Rapture when the Elect will ascend to sit on the right hand of God. Jews, Muslims and the Wrong Kind of Christians, for all their killing and dying, are only the agents, they will not ascend. 'Basically,' writes Rabbi

Richman, 'we're a doormat for them [the Rapturists] to get to their own eschatological culmination.'

Say what you like about President Bush, he has kept the Rapturists (some 15% of the American electorate) hopeful.

16. The rich want peace, the poor want justice. (Wayside pulpit)

17.   Hier verlief die Mauer.
      Sie war nicht von Dauer.

(Graffiti on a remnant of the Berlin Wall: Here ran the Wall./ It didn't last.)

David and Helen Constantine
February 2008

The Next Issue of *MPT*

The autumn issue of *Modern Poetry in Translation* (Third Series, Number 10) will be called 'The Big Green Issue'.

We want poetry, translated and original, essays, anecdotes, photographs, illustrations, all of the highest quality, treating, in whatever ways, the beauty, abundance and plight of Mother Earth. This autumn *MPT* will be truly internationalist. We want work from all quarters, out of as many languages as possible, to demonstrate an obvious fact: on Planet Earth we sink or swim together. We want the issue to be polemical, saying the things that must be said, but also celebratory, so that we see, yet again, what it is we risk losing. We want writing that will show up wrong attitudes and the deeds they encourage; but also indicate how we might live better in the living world. We borrow the Earth from our children. Good writing, world-wide, may help us return it to them in better shape.

Submissions should be sent by 1 August 2008, please, in hard copy, with return postage, to The Editors, Modern Poetry in Translation, The Queen's College, Oxford, OX1 4AW. Unless agreed in advance, submissions by email will not be accepted. Only very exceptionally will we consider work that has already been published elsewhere. Translators are themselves responsible for obtaining any necessary permissions. Since we do sometimes authorize further publication on one or two very reputable websites of work that has appeared in *MPT*, the permissions should cover that possibility.

Joe Sacco, from *Palestine*

But things weren't as cut and dry as *that* Zionist slogan. Plenty of Arabs lived in Palestine; in 1917 Arabs out-numbered Jewish inhabitants ten-to-one. But you know mathematics, it doesn't always fit into the equation:

LORD BALFOUR AGAIN

ZIONISM, BE IT RIGHT OR WRONG, GOOD OR BAD, IS ROOTED IN AGE-LONG TRADITION, IN PRESENT NEEDS, IN FUTURE HOPES, OF FAR PROFOUNDER IMPORT THAN THE DESIRE AND PREJUDICES OF 700,000 ARABS WHO NOW INHABIT THAT ANCIENT LAND.

And, incidentally:

WE DO NOT PROPOSE EVEN TO GO THROUGH THE FORM OF CONSULTING THE WISHES OF THE PRESENT INHAB-ITANTS OF THE COUNTRY.

Decision made! History follows on such heels and refugees after that... But if it's been downhill for Palestinians ever since, Israelis have soared to greater heights, who can deny it?

J. SACCO 3.92

13

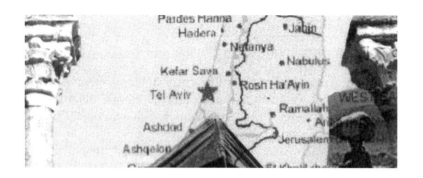

Jonathan Holmes
Israel/Palestine: a century of violence

There has never been an autonomous Palestinian State. For four centuries until 1916, the region between Aquaba in the south and Lebanon in the north, the Jordan river in the east and the Mediterranean in the west was contained within separate provinces of the Ottoman Empire.

Despite efforts by Zionist philanthropists such as Philippe de Rothschild and young zealots like David Ben-Gurion to encourage Jewish immigration to the Holy Land in the late nineteenth and early twentieth centuries, 99% of the three million Jewish émigrés from Russia and Europe between 1880 and 1914 chose to head elsewhere – mainly to America. Zionism was a booming creed, but nobody wanted to live in the desert.

World War One changed this. The Ottomans threw their lot in with Germany, and it became central to the Allied interest to undermine the vast and crumbling empire from within. Britain began openly to promote indigenous Arab independence movements as a means to this end, most famously in the expeditions of T.E.Lawrence. The Arab tribes, with no history of nationalism or centralised government, were often at variance in their agendas, a situation exploited by Westminster, where the deeper policy was to share the whole Middle East out among the victorious powers.

By the time of the final Ottoman collapse, three separate and contradictory plans had been drawn up in Europe for the future of the region. The most notorious of these was the Balfour Declaration, a grand name for a rather *ad hoc* statement by former Prime Minister Arthur Balfour. It raised the notion of a permanent Jewish settlement in what he called Palestine, a name which had little geographical meaning and by which he meant roughly somewhere between Baghdad, Sinai, Damascus and the Mediterranean.

Balfour had been influenced by British Zionists represented by Chaim Weizmann, a distinguished scientist and future first President of Israel. Simultaneously aware of Jewish interests in both the US and in the new Russian revolutionary leadership, the British government allowed the Declaration to gain valuable publicity, and ultimately a degree of continuing infamy.

At a seminal meeting of the new League of Nations at San Remo in 1920, Palestine was defined for the first time in history: it was to cover what is now Israel/Palestine, Jordan, and bits of Lebanon. In 1922, bowing to Arab pressure, the League redefined Palestine as the area west of the river Jordan and prohibited Jewish settlement anywhere else in the Middle East. At the same time, it reinforced the terms of the Balfour Declaration and stated the right of Jews to migrate to the redrawn area of Palestine, which was to be placed under British Mandate.

The Mandate of Palestine was governed from Westminster until the end of World War Two. From the beginning it pleased no one. Jews and Arabs alike resented British rule, and the Arabs resented also the influx of Jewish settlers in their land. Sporadic violence on both sides erupted throughout the interwar period, culminating in the Arab Revolt of 1936-9, to which Britain vigorously responded with the deployment of an extra 20,000 troops and much bloodshed. Despite anti-Arab feeling among the governors, in 1939 a British White Paper proposed that the future of Palestine be as an Arab state annexed to the Empire, with Jewish immigration limited to 75,000 souls over five years, a policy that remained unchanged even in the aftermath of the

Holocaust. Jewish leaders were unsurprisingly enraged, and the region was on the verge of a Jewish revolt to match the Arab one when world war once again intervened.

By 1948 the British had had enough. The garrison in Palestine was larger than that in India, placing severe strain on the post-war exchequer, and constant bilateral terrorist attacks punished both British troops and international standing. The problem was passed to the newly-formed United Nations, which voted in favour of the region's partition between a Jewish and Arab State.

On 14 May 1948 the British left and Jewish leader David Ben-Gurion immediately declared an independent state of Israel. That same day Jewish settlers swept through the desert and staked their claim in a well-orchestrated land grab. Dozens of Arab communities were forcibly appropriated, their inhabitants summarily evicted. Thousands of Arabs were made refugees, their homes occupied by the new Israelis. Those who could not flee to surrounding states were housed in temporary camps: sixty years on, their descendents still live in these same camps. The next day the surrounding Arab states attacked in a hastily formed alliance, and only a combination of Jewish desperation and Arab disorder prevented the nascent nation from being strangled at birth.

Israel survived and, after a year of struggle as much against the desert as against the indigenous population, firmly stamped its footprint on the region. For most of the ensuing decade there was an uneasy, but quiet, friction between Jews and Arabs. Developments in the Cold War meant that the Soviet Union, which had initially armed and supported Israel, shifted its attention to the Arab states in the hope that Syria and Egypt in particular might become effective clients in the region. Almost by default, this led the United States to bind itself closer to Israel in order to keep a toehold in the Middle East. Tensions rose both locally and internationally during the 1950s, reaching a peak at the Suez Crisis in 1956. This debacle led to the Israeli occupation of and subsequent withdrawal from the Sinai peninsular, the humiliation of the old colonial powers, and, as a barely noticed

side-effect, the formation of the Egyptian anti-Zionist movement
Fatah, led by Yasser Arafat.

Armed by the Russians, by the mid-sixties President Nasser of
Egypt began again to apply pressure on Israel. In Jordan, in an
attempt to unify and so control disparate Arab guerrilla attacks
on Israel, King Hussein sponsored the formation of the Palestine
Liberation Organisation, the leadership of which was soon
hijacked by Fatah and Arafat. In 1967 Nasser closed the Gulf of
Aqaba to Israeli shipping, leaving the country 'breathing with
one lung', as the Israeli defence minister put it in an appeal to the
UN. Egypt, Jordan and Syria signed a treaty of alliance against
Israel and massed their armies on the borders. Before they could
invade, the Israeli Defence Force (commanded among others by
Yitzhak Rabin and Ariel Sharon) launched a massive pre-emptive
strike on all fronts. In six days Israel defeated a coalition Arab
army at least three times its size on three borders simultaneously,
re-occupied the Sinai and the Gaza Strip, captured the segment
of Jordan known as the West Bank, and took over the Golan
Heights, previously part of Syria.

The Six-Day War was Israel's high-water mark as a military
power whilst also sowing the seeds for the next half-century of
turmoil. Instead of operating as a wholly Jewish state among
Arab nations, Israel now claimed for its own not only disputed
Arab land, but an indisputably Arab population. Until 1967 the
Palestinian problem had essentially been a refugee problem, with
thousands of displaced communities seeking redress for 1948.
From 1967 it became instead an issue of Arab statehood and
liberation. From being the controversial underdog Israel had
repositioned itself as the bully in the playground. Israel also
faced a dilemma: should it, as a democratic state, incorporate
the hostage Palestinians into the system and run the risk of
tipping the demographic balance and, in time, potentially seeing
the election of an Arab leadership, or should it suppress its new
population in a two-tier system of *de facto* apartheid? Israel chose
the latter option.

The repercussions of this were significant. The PLO and

Fatah adjusted their position and for the first time began to think in terms of an independent Palestinian nation, rather than campaigning only for the eviction of the Jews. It should be noted that at this stage the West Bank was still technically occupied Jordan: it was not until 1988 that Jordan renounced all claims to its former province. Until that date the PLO were effectively campaigning for independence from both Israel and from Jordan.

The Six-Day War was round one. Round two came in 1973, when the same Arab nations once again attacked Israel, this time with increased Russian support, in the Yom Kippur or Ramadan (depending on your religion) War. With more territory to defend and perhaps a more complacent attitude, Israel struggled to repel the invaders, and only a belated intervention by the US in the form of a massive arms drop carried the day.

The 1970s saw a further change in tack, away from the dialectic of war and ceasefire and towards a more or less constant theme of guerrilla warfare and ongoing diplomacy that continues today. Patient negotiation paid off and Israel eventually returned the Sinai to Egypt in return for president Sadat's recognition of the right of Israel to exist. This formula of 'land for peace' was later adopted by Jimmy Carter at the Camp David Accords in 1978, which, though they polarised opinion in the Arab world, crucially established both Israel and a state of Palestine as viable actual and potential entities, recognised on an international level. The price paid was Sadat's assassination and the exclusion of Egypt from the Arab League.

Peace talks continued through the early 1980s with both sides raising the stakes. Arafat relocated the PLO to Lebanon and attacked Israel from there, causing the Israelis to occupy Lebanon and expel him. Though they withdrew shortly thereafter, the antipathy they created led to the formation of Hizbollah, whose stated aim, once again, was the wholesale destruction of Israel. The increasingly hardline attitude of Israeli prime minister Yitzhak Shamir led to the first intifada in 1987, a popular Palestinian uprising later commandeered by the PLO, and which led to the formation of the more radical organisation Hamas.

Until 1989 the conflict had been influenced disproportionately by events at the global level, with both sides to some extent clients in superordinate contests, firstly in Europe and secondly between the US and Russia. The end of the Cold War gave the first opportunity for the parties themselves to talk, unencumbered by international interests, and the clandestine Oslo talks were the result. The new Israeli prime minister, Yitzhak Rabin, began secret talks with Arafat brokered by the Norwegians. Fourteen separate meetings took place in Oslo in 1994 without the knowledge of the Americans or any Arab nation. The outcome was a five-year plan for the restoration of the occupied territories, beginning with Gaza and Jericho in return for the full and total Palestinian recognition of Israel and the cessation of violence. The Oslo Accords were eventually ratified publicly at the White House with Bill Clinton, and led to the historic handshake between Nobel prizewinners Rabin and Arafat.

The honeymoon was not to last. Though Oslo provided the blueprint for all future peace plans (including the famous 'roadmap' set out in 2002 by the newly formed 'Quartet'), its most powerful architect, Yitzhak Rabin, was assassinated in 1996 by a fanatical Israeli student. Momentum was never fully regained.

The new century brought changes for the worse. An ailing Arafat's authority in Ramallah was waning, and in September 2000 Ariel Sharon (then a minister in the Barak government) openly visited the Al-Aqsa mosque, the holiest Muslim site in Jerusalem. Against a background of rising extremism in the Islamic world, this seemed a calculated insult and a second intifada, more ferocious than the first, was launched. A year later Sharon, who had fought in every Israeli war and was known as one of its most ruthless soldiers, became prime minister, while the rise of Al-Qaeda seemed to confirm the derailment of any peace plan.

Palestinian attacks increased and Sharon eventually sealed

the borders around the West Bank and Gaza. The Palestinian economy was effectively throttled, and Arafat was besieged in his Ramallah compound until his death in 2004. Sharon ordered the construction of a 'fence' to separate the West Bank from Israel proper and in 2005 unexpectedly and unilaterally gave Gaza back to the Arabs and removed all Jewish settlers, though still keeping all borders sealed. His punitive strategy toward the Palestinian people themselves led to a huge increase in both suicide bombings and mortar attacks on Israel.

In January 2006 Sharon suffered a massive heart attack and remains in a coma; he was succeeded by Ehud Olmert. Significantly, for the first time since World War Two the leadership of Israel is no longer, despite the continuing presence of 85-year-old Shimon Peres, dominated by veterans of the 1948 war. After Arafat's death the Palestinian administration was forced to become more plural, and Hamas became a major player alongside Fatah, now run by Mahmoud Abbas. In 2006, in free elections, Hamas trounced Fatah and became the government of Palestine. Abbas and the international community rejected this outcome due to Hamas' terrorist base and refusal to recognise Israel. After attempts at collaboration and all-out conflict among Palestinians, the situation became one of political stalemate, with the Palestinian people themselves still suffering significant privation due to Israeli blockades and attacks.

January 2008 saw the launch of a new peace initiative led by George Bush, one which was clearer than ever in its stated aims of an independent Palestine at pre-1967 borders and a full acceptance of Israel. Exactly sixty years after Israel's creation, it remains to be seen whether this will be more successful than nearly a century of previous attempts at reconciliation.

Mahmoud Darwish
'Mural'
Translated by Rema Hammami
and John Berger

My nurse says: you are better now
and injects me with a tranquillizer:
Be calm
and worthy of what you're about to dream
even a little . . .

I saw my French doctor
open my prison cell
and beat me with a stick
assisting him were two local policemen

I saw my father return
from the Hajj
fainted from the Hijazi sunstroke
he said to the flock of angels surrounding him:
Extinguish me!

I saw Moroccan boys playing soccer
pelting me with stones:
Pass your word back-scram!
and leave us our mother
O father trespassing in the cemetery!

I saw René Char
sitting with Heidegger
two metres away from me
I saw them drinking wine
not looking for poetry
The dialogue was a ray of light
And there was a passer-by waiting

I saw three comrades weeping
as they were sewing me a shroud
with gold thread

I saw Ma'ari expel his critics
from his poem
I'm not blind
to see what you all see
Vision is a light that leads to nothingness...or madness

I saw countries embrace my good mornings saying:
Be worthy of the bread's aroma
May the flowers of the pavement make you elegant
There's still fire on your mother's hearth
And the welcome is as warm as bread!

Green
The land of my poem is green
One stream is enough to make me whisper to the butterfly:
O sister
One stream is enough to solder the ancient myths onto the
    falcon's wing as it swaps
banners for distant peaks
there where armies have founded for me a kingdom of
    oblivion
There is no nation smaller than its poem
But weapons make words too big for the living
and the dead who inhabit the living
And letters make the sword on the dawn's belt glitter
till the desert becomes parched for songs or drowns in them

No life is long enough for me to join my end to my
    beginning
The shepherds took my story and hid it in the grass
covering the magic debris where the tents once stood
and like this with trumpets and choral rhymes they cheated
    oblivion
then left me the hoarseness of memory on the stone of
    farewell
and they didn't return . . .

Pastoral our days are pastoral between city and tribe
I can't find a secret night for your saddle studded with
    mirages
You said to me: without you why do I need a name?
Call me
for I created you when you named me
and you killed me once you owned the name
How could you kill me?
Me the outcast of all this night
Let me enter the forest of your desire
Embrace me, hold me, squeeze me till

I shed pure nuptial honey on the hive
Scatter me with the breeze in your hands then gather me up
The night renders up its soul to you Intruder
and a star can't see me without knowing how my family will
    kill me with rosewater
So give me the sudden happiness that needs me
and I will break my jar with my own hands

You suggest I change my path?
I didn't say anything – my life is beyond me
I'm the me saying:
The last poem fell from my date palms
I travel within myself
besieged by contradictions
And life is worth the candle of its mystery
and its prophetic birds

I wasn't born to know I was going to die
but to love what's in God's shadow
Beauty takes me to the beautiful
And I love your love
freed from itself and its signs

I am my alternative
I am the one who says to himself:
From the smallest things are born the largest thoughts
Rhythm doesn't come from the words
but from the joining of two bodies in a long night . . .

I'm the one talking to himself to tame memory . . . are you
    me?
You, me and the third which is the two of us
fluttering between and declaring, don't forget!
O our death! Take us then
so we can learn to shine…
On me there's no sun or moon

I left my gloom hanging on a branch of a boxthorn
and the place weighed less
as my fugitive spirit took to the sky

I'm the me saying:
O girl: what did the longed-for ones do to you?
The breeze ruffles and carries us like autumn scents
My wife you grew on my crutches
And sure of what you see, they will help you on the
     Damascus Road
A guardian angel and two doves fly over what's left of our
     lives
And the land is a festival . . .

The land is a festival of the vanquished and we are among
     them
It's we who brought the anthem here
camping in the wind like an old eagle's feather
We were good and pious without Christ's teachings
and stronger than the grass at summer's end
You are my truth and I your question
We have inherited nothing but our names
and you are my playground and I your shade
at the crossroads of the anthem

We weren't there when the saints and their magic and malice
     got into the anthem
On the horns of a mountain goat they carried the place from
     its time to another time
It would have been more natural if the stars in our sky were a
     fraction higher than the stones in our well
and the prophets less nagging
then the soldiers could have heard our praises

Green
The land of my poem is green
The song carries her as she was
fertile from past to past
And I have of her: Narcissus contemplating the water of his
    image
And I have of her: the sharpness of shadows in synonyms and
    the exactitude of meaning . . .
And I have of her: what is common in the sayings of prophets
    on the roof of the night
And I have of her: the donkey of wisdom abandoned on a
    hill, mocking her legends and her reality . . .
And I have of her: the symbols stuffed with opposites
Realism doesn't find memories
Abstraction doesn't lead to illumination
My other self I have of her
Singers can only inscribe her days in a diary:
If the dream isn't enough
I'll be heroically sleepless at the door of exile
And I have of her: the echo of my language from the walls
removing salt from the sea
at the very moment when my strong heart betrays me

Higher than the valley was my wisdom
When I told the devil: No, don't test me!
Don't give me your either-ors
Leave me in the Old Testament climbing to heaven
there is my kingdom
Take hold of history O son of my father
take history and make with guesses what you need

And I have tranquillity
A small grain of wheat will be enough for us
for me and my brother the enemy
Since my hour hasn't yet come
nor the hour of the harvest
I must embrace absence, listen to my heart and follow it
to Kana in Galilee
My hour has not yet come
Perhaps something in myself rejects me
Perhaps I am someone else
The figs are not yet ripe around the girls' dresses
and from the feather of the ostrich I have not yet been born
Nobody is waiting for me there
I have come before and I have come after
I find nobody who believes what I see
I the one who sees
am far away
The faraway

My me who are you?
We are two on the road
and one at the resurrection
Take me to the light of my disappearance to see how I'll be
    in my other mirror
Who my me will I be after you?
Is my body behind me or before you?
Who am I you tell me?
Make me as I make you
anoint me with almond oil
crown me with cedar
and transport me from the valley to a white eternity
Teach me life on the way
test me like an atom in the heavens
come to my aid against the boredom of the eternal
and be lenient when the roses pierce from my veins and
    wound me . . .

Our hour has not yet come
No prophet counts time with a fistful of late grass
Has time closed its circle?
No angels visit the place so poets can leave their past behind
    on the dusk's horizon
and open by hand their tomorrows
Sing again Anat darling goddess
my first poem about genesis
Storytellers have already found the willow's birth certificate
    in the autumn stone
and shepherds their well in the depth of a song
And time has already come for those who play with meaning
on a butterfly's wing caught in rhymes

So sing darling goddess
I am both the prey Anat and the arrows
I am words
the funeral oration the call of the muezzin
and the martyr

I haven't said goodbye to the ruins yet
So don't be what I was except once
once was enough to see how time collapses itself like a
    bedouin tent
in a wind from the north
How places split apart and the what-has-gone wears the litter
    of a deserted temple
Everything around me looks like me
and I look like nothing here
As if the earth is too small for the lyrically sick
descendents of the poor crazy devils who when they had a
    good dream
taught love poetry to a parrot
and saw all frontiers open . . .

I want to live . . .
I have work to do on deck
not to save birds from our famines or sea sickness
But to study the deluge close-up
And after?
What do survivors do with the ancient land?
Do they take up the same story?
How did it begin?
What's the epilogue?
No one comes back from death to tell us the truth . . .

Wait for me Death beyond the earth
Wait for me on your land
until I finish my talk with what's left of my life
not far from your tent
Wait for me till I finish reading Tarafa bin al Abed

The existentialists who drew up from the well of each
      moment
freedom
justice
the wine of the gods...
they seduce me

So wait Death till I have settled the funeral arrangements in
      the clear spring of my birth
and have forbidden the orators to lyricise again
about the sad land and the steadfastness of figs and olives in
      the face of time's armies
Dissolve me I'd say in all the femininity of the letter 'nuun'
Let me gulp down the Sura of the Merciful in the Qur'an
And walk with me in my ancestors' footsteps
silently to the rhythm of a flute
towards my eternity
And don't place a violet on my grave
it's the flower of the depressed

and reminds the dead of how love died too young
Place seven ears of green wheat on my coffin and a few red
    anemones should you find them
otherwise leave the church roses for churches and newly-weds

Wait till I pack my bag Death
my toothbrush soap after-shave and some clothes
Is the climate warm over there?
Do the seasons change in the eternal whiteness?
Or does the weather stay fixed in autumn or winter?
Will one book be enough to read in non-time?
Or should I take a library?
And what do they talk over there?
vernacular or classical?

Death wait for me Death
till I clear my mind in Spring
and regain my health
Then you'll be the noble hunter who doesn't kill the gazelle
    while it's drinking

Let's be friendly and open together
I'll give you my well-filled life
and you give me a view of the planets
No one exactly dies
Rather souls change their looks and address
Death my shadow who will lead me
you the third in two
you hesitant colour of sapphires and topaz
you blood of the peacock
you poacher of a fox's heart
you, our delirium!
Sit
Put down your hunting things outside under the awning
Hang your set of heavy keys above the door!

You Mighty One stop looking at my veins monitoring the
    last drop
you are mightier than medicine
mightier than the respirator
mightier than pungent honey
You don't need to kill me – my sickness will
Why not be nobler than the insects?
Be transparently yourself
a visible message to be read by the invisible
Be like love – a storm among trees
don't stand on the threshold like a beggar or tax collector
Don't be an undercover policeman directing traffic
Be strong like shining steel and take off the fox's mask
Be chivalrous glamorous fatal
Say what you want to say:
I come from one meaning and go to another
Life is liquid
and I thicken it and define it
with my pair of scales and sceptre
Death wait
take a seat
drink a glass of wine
and don't bargain with me
Someone like you doesn't bargain with anyone
and someone like me doesn't argue with the herald of the
    invisible

Take it easy – perhaps you're worn out by star wars
Who am I that you should visit me?
Have you time to check out my poem?
No that's not your concern
your concern is with the clay of man's being
not with what he does or says
You're defeated Death by the arts by each one of them
You're defeated by the songs of the land of two rivers
by the Egyptian obelisk by the tomb of the Pharaohs

in the temples there are bas-reliefs who defeated you
And eternity escaped through your cracks
So carry on with yourself
and with us
as you see fit

And I want
I want to live
I have work to do on the geography of volcanoes
From desolation to ruin
from the time of Lot to Hiroshima
As if I'd never yet lived
with a lust I've still to know
Perhaps Now has gone further away
and yesterday come closer
So I take Now's hand to walk along the hem of history
and avoid cyclic time
with its chaos of mountain goats
How can my tomorrow be saved?
By the velocity of electronic time
or by my desert caravan slowness?
I have work till my end
as if I won't see tomorrow
and I have work for today who isn't here
So I listen
softly softly
to the ant beat of my heart: Bear with me my patience
I hear the cry of the imprisoned stone: Set my body free
in a violin I see yearning's migration between peat and sky
and in my feminine hand
I hold tight my familiar eternity:
I was created then loved then died then awoke on the grass of
    my tombstone
whose letters from time to time refer to me
What's the use of spring if it doesn't please the dead
and show them the joy of life and the shock of forgetfulness?

That's the clue to my poems
at least the sentimental ones
And what on earth are dreams if not our only way of
    speaking?

Take your time Death
Take a seat on the crystal of my days
as if you've always been a constant friend
as if you were the foreigner among living creatures
You are the exile
you haven't a life
your life is only my death
you neither live nor die
you kidnap children between their thirst for milk and milk
You'll never be a child in a cradle rocked by finches
never will angels and stags tease you with their horns
as they teased us
we guests of the butterfly
You are the miserable exile
with no woman pressing you to her breasts
no woman to make during the long night
nostalgia Two
in the language of desire
and to make into One
the land and heaven which is in us
No boy of yours to say: Father I love you
You are the exile

You king of kings
There's no praise for your sceptre
no falcon waiting on your horse
no pearls embedded in your crown
You are stripped of flags and music
How can you go around like a cowardly thief without guards
    or singers?
Who do you think you are?

You're the Great Highness of Death
mighty leader of the invincible Assyrians

So do with us
and yourself
as you see fit

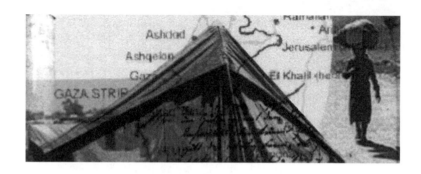

Deema Shehabi
Two ghazals

Ghazal

If I die, leave the balcony open
                    Federico Garcia Lorca

Feet, young and old, tumble by then flee when the balcony
    opens,
but what about the house that seethes when the balcony
    opens?

Angels with daggers march through the funeral air of burned
children, and you're in the witness seat when the balcony
    opens.

I want to watch those voluptuous watermelons prune the ash,
says one angel, so for God's sake keep clear when the balcony
    opens.

We can't defend this pillow plump with insults, so we beat it
  down
before the jasmine convenes when the balcony opens.

Without the soil in Palestine, I'm bereft of planting,
soil of succulent green beans, darkly fleeting when the
  balcony opens.

The hour of magic cats dressed in lavender draws near;
look toward the horizon and halt your weave when the
  balcony opens.

Says Ondaatje: my love, punctual in green silk, brushes my
  face
with cinnamon and blurs it into my cheek when the balcony
  opens.

Let's double the batch of thyme bread before its scent pierces
  the earth,
before the dead hunger-heave when the balcony opens.

O brother, why not enter this room solidly with our right
  foot, ignoring
our torturers, as we fall to our knees when the balcony opens?

Transcendent poet, how will you tiptoe past a walled-in
  nation
that tramples the lapis lazuli when the balcony opens?

Pain dominates, says the father, but your smile bargains with
  that devil,
and lightens loads for dreams when the balcony opens.

My sister ruffles the sky, cries the boy in the jeep, and my
    brother lies motionless
beside me, but my body will burst into stream when the
    balcony opens.

O love, the length of your rib cage is my given fortune. Look
    how the twilight
disrobes as I measure your needs when the balcony opens.

Ghazal
(for Marilyn Hacker)

Your night is of lilac
                Mahmoud Darwish

Who crosses the road at night in shawls of lilac?
Again, we'll lash out at the future with all our lilac.

The girl wails over her father's body on a beach hiving
with warships as though she's dressed in fireballs of lilac.

Laila, bitten by ferocious longing, absorbs the oiled blood
of Qays' jasmine, measures the deep-carved sprawl of his
    lilac.

O lover of the tabla, your beat swelling with multitudes,
come rest your blue-veined hands on the scripted calls of
    lilac.

I will return one day, she says, to light the lamp of my
    snuffed-
out country, to translate the original protocol of lilac.

The Sufis say that everyone is to blame in a time of war while
they row their night boat towards waterfalls of lilac.

Shahid, how often did you 'land on ashen tarmacs'
landing – then flying – your feet hauled by lilac?

Nothing is left for this parched earth where you are buried,
says the groom to his bride, except a rainfall of lilac.

If you don't let my son return to his mother, says the father
to the interrogator, your body will be mauled by lilac.

How we betrayed those summer clouds that crumpled our
    bed sheets;
our hasty unfolding, our constant footfalls towards lilac.

What have we lost, father, that can't be regained? What of
    our devotional
yearning beneath the overgrown walls of lilac?

I don't want to break the dusk from where I stand, the
    martyr says. The grass is
too musky today, and the air enthrals with lilac.

Marilyn Hacker
Two ghazals

Ghazal: *Dar al-harb*
(for Wafa'a Zeinal'abidin)

I might wish, like any citizen, to celebrate my country
but millions have reason to fear and hate my country.

I might wish to write, like Virginia: as a woman, I have none,
but women and men are crushed beneath its weight: my
    country.

As English is my only mother tongue,
it's in English I must excoriate my country.

The good ideas of Marx or Benjamin Franklin
do not excuse the gulags, or vindicate my country.

Who trained the interrogators, bought the bulldozers?
– the paper trails all indicate my country.

It used to be enough to cross an ocean
and view, as a bemused expatriate, my country.

The June blue sky, the river's inviting meanders:
then a letter, a headline make me contemplate my country.

Is my only choice the stupid lies of empire
or the sophistry of apartheid: my country?

Walter Benjamin died in despair of a visa
permitting him to integrate my country.

Exiles, at least, have clarity of purpose:
can say my town, my mother and my fate, my country.

There used to be a face that looked like home,
my interlocutor or my mate, my country.

Plan your resistance, friends, I'll join you in the street,
but be circumspect, don't underestimate my country.

Where will justice and peace get the forged passports
it seems they'll need to infiltrate my country?

Eggplant and peppers, shallots, garlic and cumin:
let them be, married on my plate, my country.

Ghazal: *Min al-hobbi ma khatal*
(for Deema Shehabi)

You, old friend, leave, but who releases me from the love that
    kills?
Can you tell the love that sets you free from the love that
    kills?

No mail again today. The retired diplomat
stifles in the day's complacency from the love that kills.

What once was home is across what once was a border
which exiles gaze at longingly from the love that kills.

The all-night dancer, the mother of four, the tired young doctor
all contracted HIV from the love that kills.

There is pleasure, too, in writing easy, dishonest verses.
Nothing protects your poetry from the love that kills.

The coloratura keens a triumphant swan-song
as if she sipped an elixir of glee from the love that kills.

We learn the maxim: 'So fine the thread,
so sharp the necessity' from the love that kills.

The calligrapher went blind from his precision
and yet he claims he learned to see from the love that kills.

Spare me, she prays, from dreams of the town I grew up in,
from involuntary memory, from the love that kills.

Homesick soldier, do you sweat in the glare of this checkpoint
to guard the homesick refugee from the love that kills?

Jack Hamesh
Two letters from Palestine to
Ingeborg Bachmann
Translated by David Constantine

Ingeborg Bachmann describes her meeting and friendship with
Jack Hamesh in her 'War Diary' which we published, translated
by Mike Lyons, in *MPT* 3/3, summer 2005. An Austrian Jew,
Hamesh escaped to England (though already aged 18) on a
Kindertransport in 1938. He came back to Austria with the British
Army in 1945, working for Field Security, and in that capacity
interviewed the eighteen-year-old Bachmann, in a way she felt
to be hostile and sarcastic. But soon they were close friends.
He became a welcome guest in her family home in the Gailtal,
outside Klagenfurt. She describes him as 'small, a bit ugly,
glasses'. Their friendship flourished very quickly in a shared love
of literature and ideas. Because of the war she had been starved
of such conversation. She wrote in her diary, 'This is the loveliest
summer of my life, and if I live to be a hundred this spring and
summer will still be the loveliest.' Hamesh seems to have left
Carinthia, for Palestine, badly smitten with Bachmann, in the
early summer of 1946. These two letters are the fullest he wrote
to her and the second of them is the last that has been preserved.
Whether the correspondence ceased then, is not known. Every

effort has been made to trace Jack Hamesh and any family he might have in Israel, but so far without success.

24.7.1946

My dear, dear Inge,

Finally I can write a few lines to you. Since I was forced to leave you I have not had a moment's quiet. You can't imagine how much I suffered on the journey from your beautiful Carinthia to Palestine.

Now almost a month has passed and still I haven't managed to compose myself.

I've had hard times to get through in my life but it seems to me that nothing of what I have experienced before can compare with these last days and weeks.

A complete uprooting, a disorientation such as I have never lived through before, the time just past was for me the worst in all my experience. Dear, kind Inge, forgive me for writing such words, how I should love to tell you cheerful things but with every line I write comes new grief and new pain. I cannot even describe to you my real condition, I feel as though I had sunk to an infinite depth, a catastrophe that perhaps only I can feel, for I alone am experiencing it, and I am more alone than I ever was before, not even the death of my dear mother shook me quite so much as this last month has done. Alas, at present I can tell you very little for I am still in a state in which I can't begin anything and beginning is not easy here. No accommodation, no work, no prospect of any improvement. But one thing is clear to me already, I shall have to work very hard, at the start I shall have to accept any sort of job if I am to survive at all. Life in the army has done nothing to prepare me for this struggle. The place upsets all my plans, I'm confronted by completely new conditions and by facts I could not have foreseen. Day by day it becomes clearer and clearer to me how decisive the step I have just taken is.

Forgive me for not telling you anything about my journey and nothing about my life itself, I can't do it. I am in such an agitated state and for now at least can't decide on anything. But I think of you, dearest Inge, constantly. Not a day goes by without my looking at your picture which is still in that book of yours that I leaf through now and then. For I'm still not able to read and who knows when I'll be capable of viewing and judging things a bit more calmly.

Where now are the days in your lovely room together and in your beautiful garden? Again and again I remember those wonderful hours and even now I can hardly write, one single thought of you and your dear house and home brings tears to my eyes.

It is terrible to live alone and especially when you have to leave people behind whom you have grown to love, and that I grew to love you, and to honour and esteem you, you must surely have felt.

Only one thing still hurts me. You didn't say a single word about seeing each another again or about staying or meeting again one day somewhere. I know it will be difficult but the hope that it may happen one day should have made us speak of it. Even at that last moment on the main street when I ran towards you weeping when our car had driven past you, even then you said nothing and, dear Inge, I should so like to have heard it from your lips, We shall see each other again.

Remember me to your dear little sister, I saw her on the last day when I was saying a fond goodbye to the Pirker family, I couldn't look her in the eyes because if I had . . .

And my good wishes to your dear mother and father also, tell them I always felt well and happy in their house and in their company, tell them that whatever may have happened, whatever things I suffered in Austria, I and thousands of others, it will never make me forget the friendship and kindness I felt in your house.

Dearest Inge, remember me to Elisabeth and other people who were kind to me.

But above all, my dear Inge, I send my love to you and assure you that my thoughts are always with you and that in you I

found someone I shall never forget unless it should be that you
no longer wished to hear from me. My situation today is bad and
tomorrow it will be worse. Please think of your Jacky so that I
may have at least that comfort.

Jack

My good wishes to the Pirkers   Write back soon.
    Letter on the way. And to the Erbers.

Tel-Aviv, 16 July 1947

Dear Inge,

Finally our tired correspondence has recovered a little
momentum! Of course I do understand that time and
circumstances may often cause an interruption, but no matter. I
am all the more pleased if you have still not forgotten that you
have a distant friend who is always glad to hear from you, still
thinks of you and still wishes to see you again.

Your letter was lovely, but not only that, it was honest,
expansive, open, friendly and intelligent. When I read your lines
I can't help admiring you again. Not many girls of your age
would be able to handle the times and their problems as you do.
You have learned from these years of trial and have progressed
in your thinking and in your humanity, whereas most of your
contemporaries have stood still and – what is worse – now they
never will develop.

You precious last letter arrived a few days before your birthday.
Believe me, on 25 June I was there with you at home, in your
lovely house, sitting again with you, your dear mother and father
and with Isi and Heinzi, in a joyful mood, deep in an interesting
conversation, happy. It was easy to imagine, I put myself back
in the year 1946 and wholly forgot that in the meantime twelve
long months have passed. I really did manage it! I sent you a
telegram a few days before your birthday. I hope it reached you
in time. I sent it home because I assumed that you would at least
celebrate your coming of age with your parents and brother and
sister.

But again your drive for independence prevailed and you stayed in Vienna, you wanted to face that rite of passage alone and in loneliness.

I will try in this letter to write less about general political and social problems and more about myself, my surroundings, my leisure, Palestine, the people here and various other things that will interest you.

If you ask me am I content or even happy, then to the first I answer yes but to the second a decided no. I am content because any man these days if he has work and can feed himself from it and needn't get on anyone else's nerves, that is, needn't be a burden on those around him, he can and must be content. I have already had several jobs here. In a leather factory and in an office, in the fields and as a waiter. At the moment I'm trying to get the brick machine going that I told you about in Austria. Of course the difficulties are considerable. You have to be able to do everything here to keep your head above water. The attitude towards work is utterly unlike that in Europe. Needless to say, my mother dreamed quite different dreams. But who ever reckoned with such a collapse of all our traditional bourgeois ideas? With such an upheaval of the way things were? Who could comprehend the vast decline and fall of mind and culture? Who in 1938 would ever have thought to see a child wandering alone in the world solely for the reason that he was born a Jew? Who could have believed that precisely those responsible for the upbringing and education of children, their fathers and mothers, would perish wretchedly in some gas chamber or other? It was a cruel time, a time that even today we can scarcely comprehend. So violent were the shocks and blows, so unbelievably much rained down on us in those years. For that reason I am content, I might easily be rotting in a mass grave in Poland or Germany or even in my OLD HOMELAND Austria.

But I am not happy. I have lost much of the joy of life, that people my age should be full of. I am alone a good deal. True, I have found myself some friends, mostly Viennese like me. But they have all suffered things such as I have, or even worse. They can't be cheerful any more either, we try to forget, sink into silence and so bury ourselves all the deeper in the unforgettable past. Who can forget his parents? His brothers and sisters and friends? Who can forget his homeland? Dear Inge, do you understand all that? Does it make you impatient that I write to you about it?

I can change the subject, but then I should write nothing more about myself. Should have to be dishonest, let the thought-machine run and simply turn off my feelings. But then I wouldn't be myself . . . But we have to live as human beings. Every other attitude is false and leads to the most nonsensical things. We have lived through them, have we not? War, hatred, race-theories and various other achievements of the twentieth century, not the least among them being the ATOM BOMB which, you will agree, is itself not a very life-affirming thing for the youth of today. For that reason I engage positively in the struggle for life, and don't just dream of all I might have been, how many opportunities I have missed, all the things I might have achieved if the years 1938-45 had never been. But those years are a reality, they have stamped us and me with their mark.

And so I work, am glad that I can feed and clothe myself decently. I don't go without. I read, study, go to concerts and the cinema, often laugh and dance. As far as possible, I make use of all that has been achieved in the way of civilization and culture. I go with the times, so to speak, but when necessary go against them too, for that also is important, especially nowadays.

It was not easy to fit in again. But I have managed that much. The soldier in me is dead. Perhaps I never was a proper soldier, as you will no doubt have noticed. I always tried to keep the human in me from shrivelling up, otherwise I might have acted quite differently in the position and capacity that were mine in Hermagor and Austria.

Palestine, in the sense it has today, is a new and awakening land. And like any country beginning to feel its strength, Palestine has enormous difficulties to overcome. This small country has advanced willynilly into the centre of world politics. Many people don't wish to accept that.

There is oil here, the Suez canal, the way to India. Jerusalem, here Christ was born, here the Jews once lived, here the Arabs have vegetated for centuries in a wretchedness you would scarcely believe possible. Here the Ten Commandments were revealed, all come as pilgrims here who believe in God, be He Christ, Jehovah or Allah. As you see, the interconnections are not uncomplicated. I am not religious, you know that as well as I do. I'm just trying to explain the historical background to the problem of the Jews. Since they were driven out of Palestine and forced to live in the Diaspora, the Jews always had one hope, the return to the land promised them by God. Of all the ancient peoples only the Jews remained. But here I have to bring in religion. The Jews were the first to believe in one god and one only. The Ten Commandments were the legal basis, the spirit was nourished by the Torah or the Book of Teachings (the Bible).

Zionism, which nowadays seeks the return of the Jews to Palestine, does not have its basis solely in that traditional longing of the Jews. There are more important reasons which go much deeper. The impossibility of assimilation, the eternal antisemitism, that most ancient of evils, the rootlessness and homelessness of the Jews, the unhealthy social and economic arrangements of the Jews among different peoples, and finally Hitler and Nazi-Germany, these have given Zionism its material and shown it the only possible way. (I shan't write any more about it. If you have any questions I'll always be glad to answer them in detail.)

The population consists of 1,200,000 Arabs (that isn't an exact figure because it is hard to carry out a count among the Arabs since a large part of them still live as nomads), 700,000 Jews and 70,000 Christians. The languages of the country are Arabic and Hebrew which unlike ancient Latin or Greek has become a living language again. English is taught in the schools as a second language. Tel-Aviv is the largest city. 250,000 inhabitants. Thirty years ago there was a sand hill there, on it now stands Tel-Aviv, which translated means Hill of Spring. Agriculture is modern, mechanized, the village more resembles the town than it does in Europe. The rural population has not fallen behind, it consists mainly of former students, middle-class people and intellectuals. Agriculture is mostly organized in collective units. The young people growing up here are strong and good-looking, proud and straightforward, simple and free from all the persecution and inferiority complexes that characterize young Jews in Europe.

We have a sub-tropical climate, which is to say there are hotter places on earth. But from June to October here too it is often oppressively hot. But the climate has not inhibited the development of the country. New villages spring up out of the sand. Water is sought and found again and again, new springs to drive back the desert. Trees are being planted on land neglected for thousands of years. Schools, libraries, evening classes, workers' study groups, trade unions, conservatories, a university, technical colleges, everything that belongs in a modern world is slowly but surely being developed here. The Arabs' standard of living has been improved a hundredfold and it is a lie when people say their land is being taken from them by the Jews. Not one single Arab has had to leave his land. On the contrary, since the arrival of the Jews the Arab population has increased, hospitals, arrangements for better hygiene, maternity care, these are all the pioneering work of the once homeless, outcast and detested Jews.

There is no winter here such as we know in Europe. But from October till the beginning of June here too there is cloud, rain, thunder and lightning. Very very rarely snow. In Jerusalem it was a sensation a few years ago when children were able to throw snowballs. Tel-Aviv is modern in the truest sense of the word. Architecture, clothing, the tempo of life etc. You find the same things here, good and bad, as you would in any large town. Jerusalem is more conservative, quieter. On

Saturdays you really might think you were living in a holy
city. You don't see a single car. Haifa is the harbour town. Very
beautifully situated, better than Tel-Aviv since it stretches
along the slopes of a hill.

In Jerusalem there are Jews and Arabs, in Haifa too, in Tel-
Aviv only Jews. The girls here dress very tastefully. Nothing
extravagant. The men during the day mostly in shorts. Evenings
mostly in well-cut long trousers and white or other monochrome
shirts. Without ties. You can't tell their social origins from
the way people dress. The coffee houses are very lively. In the
evenings people go in their thousands to the seafront for cold
drinks and Viennese music. A great deal of music is listened
to here. Concert halls always full. Among the great names
the best-loved are Mozart, Schubert, Beethoven, then Chopin,
Tchaikovsky, Dvorak, Smetana – Ravel too and a few local
newcomers in music are extremely popular.

As you see, dear Inge, Palestine lives despite everything. Here
the Jews are being given their last chance. For at least so long as
the other peoples cannot renounce their hatred of the Jews this
is the only place where the Jews surviving in Europe can find
refuge and a new life.

I had a lot more to write to you. But the letter is too long
already. There were several things in your letter I wanted to
answer but it's too late for today. I'll wait for your reply and
then I'll write again at greater length.

Please write soon and lots. Everything, everything interests
me. About you and your parents and Isi and Heinzi. About
Austria, Vienna and the beautiful Gailtal where probably you
are now.

With warmest good wishes, yours in friendship
Jack

[The following paragraph, like the whole of the previous letter, is handwritten.]

Dear Inge,

Don't be cross that I typed this instead of writing. I thought it would make reading much easier for you. Don't think me rude or disrespectful. I had so much to write and with the typewriter it is much clearer and more definite.

So don't be cross, my dear Inge.

[On the back of the envelope: J. Hamesh Y.Nagarastr. 6. Tel-Aviv PALESTINE. And postmarked twice: Tel-Aviv 16 July 47 Registered]

Agi Mishol
'Parent Poems'
Translated by Vivian Eden

The daughter of Holocaust survivors, Agi Mishol was born in Transylvania in 1947 to a Hungarian-speaking family and emigrated to Israel with her parents at the age of 4. She lives in an agricultural community and is the mother of two children. She has published more than 10 books of poetry. Her latest, *Things Happen*, is a retrospective selection that has followed *Selected and New Poems* (2003) – a comprehensive volume that has sold more then 10,000 copies, an extraordinary number. A caring mentor of many young poets, she teaches at Alma College and is currently the Poet in Residence at the Hebrew University in Jerusalem. Her book *Look There*, translated by Lisa Katz, was published in U.S (2006) by Graywolf Press. *The Swimmers*, a bilingual volume of her poetry, was published by Poetry Ireland (1998). Her poems have also been translated into Arabic, French, German and other languages and have appeared in anthologies around the world. She is much in demand for lectures and readings and her poems have been set to music and performed by various artists. She has been artistic director of the International Poets Festival at Mishkenot Shaananim in Jerusalem and has represented Israel at literary events in the United States, Germany, Macedonia, Turkey, Ireland and elsewhere. As a translator she has brought

the work of Irish, British, American and Australian poets into
Hebrew. 'Parent Poems' are part of a cycle completed after a visit
to her birthplace, which is now in Romania.

1

Every night you spread a white sheet
and surrender.
One lamp illuminates you both
but each of you is strict about your own side.
On your chest of drawers, Papa, there are Ventolin
and the inhaler.
On yours, Mama, the pocket encyclopedia,
the Hungarian-Hebrew Dictionary
and the Book of Psalms with a photo of your parents
between the pages, wandering from chapter to chapter.
Your head, Papa, rests on a mountain of pillows
with a small flowered cushion at the summit
while you, Mama, make do with only two.
When the light goes out you turn back to back,
wrapping yourselves in the goose-down quilt
you brought on the boat from Transylvania.

2

Papa, you taught me to recite 'Der Erlkönig'
in German
and to play on our piano 'The Acacia Path'
that every Hungarian has trod.
And Mama, you taught me to baste and to iron
and all the prepositions in Latin
you'd managed to learn before they took you away.
You didn't know any stories, Papa, but
we laughed at a lot of dirty jokes

transformed into fairy tales for children
while, Mama, you remembered one tale from Grimm.
Papa, you taught me to ride a bike
and all the operettas from the merry days of Vienna
and Mama, you had 'a weak organism' –
the perforated abyss of sadness because of which
with me, everything is always perfectly fine.

Alan Hart
'Volunteer 1969'

Accident or fate took me to Israel in 1969. I worked in Harrods and then set out to hitchhike to India. I got to Greece before I ran out of money and had a dream of Palestine – maybe Lawrence of Arabia was behind this. Anyway I sold some blood and got a ship for Lebanon, planning to cross. I was put off in Cyprus, having no visa or money, and after a few days virtually penniless found a Turkish ship for Haifa where I fell in with a couple of other individuals and we were all greeted by a man from Kibbitz Kabri looking for volunteers. There followed the best few months of youth, learning about the world and meeting people who were converts or searchers or like myself rather cast adrift. I found the Israelis on the kibbutz a mixture of fierce, kind and inscrutable, there was some talk of the still recent war and arms sales and so on, but mostly it was hard work and silence. The only poem I started was at the crusader castle of Montfort, which I didn't finish for a few years. I paid for the return passage by working in a factory before going to university. I wrote 'Volunteer 1969' in response to reading *MPT* and thinking about those days as well as recent events and pictures of Kabri seen on the Internet. I've never stopped thinking about that time, and I became over the years a passionate reader about Judaism and Jewish poetry and the Holocaust, as well as a student of Buddhism and Christianity.

There are a couple of references in the poem to Elaine Feinstein's 'Scattering'. I was not sent by anyone to Israel, and was not expected by anyone, least of all my mother, to go there. A family legend of Jewish blood has not been substantiated. The question of who has a right to Palestine, Israel or the Arabs, obviously lurks behind the poem. I can't imagine there not being an Israel, but there are of course skeletons in the cupboard referred to here.

Volunteer 1969

The wind whistles in the unused chimney.
I half-close one eye and I see Palestine –
A man I was once, one in a long line, him and me.

You could start anywhere with this piece,
On the beach near Ashkelon with dogs perhaps,
One wild night returning from Jericho, somewhat overshot
    my place.

Large Carlos who always drove a tractor,
Or the battlements of Acre, hurrying through tunnels,
A man with a machete, the slice and then comes the banana
    factor.

In another we see you wrestling on the floor.
You so wanted to borrow a radio to listen to Brahms.
You couldn't abide the barren absence any more.

In version four we meet John Brown, your Jerusalem
    companion
The second time: we spent the night in a graveyard.
John really existed because you met him in Tokyo many
    years on.

He remembered you and thus corroborated
Your existence there, the truth of the myth,
Because after all it seemed fated.

It was a dream you had in Greece that made you go,
A dream of Palestine; there was no plan at all,
No one sent you and you couldn't know

That there at the jetty would be a man looking for new
    recruits
To take to the top of Mount Carmel
And introduce to new humus and fresh fruits

Before setting out for the border, pointing down and asking
    maybe
What was that domed place. You were nothing then,
Neither Jew nor Christian, not Buddhist, altogether free.

Before words you got up and went to work with your team,
Only later breakfasting on tomato and avocado.
Then at eleven o'clock sharp from the sea the breeze came.

The immaculate border with Lebanon where the sun always
    shone.
The walk one Sabbath to the Crusader castle of Montfort,
The late way back past Arab shepherds tripping on fields of
    stone.

In no time you were fit enough to trot
With a bunch of bananas on either shoulder – never
Again would you be so strong, so young, so – what?

This morning looking, picking at what little is known
Of the history of Al Kabri, you remembered a kind
Of museum. A row at least of photos you were shown.

The only survival of 48. Palestine.
I never doubted that Israel would survive.
But no one sent me there. The idea was mine.

Rows of books collected since that heaven.
None say Palestine, and come to think of it,
None say Israel either, though several do say Hebrew,
Jewish, Yiddish, and one says
Tel-Aviv, 1947.

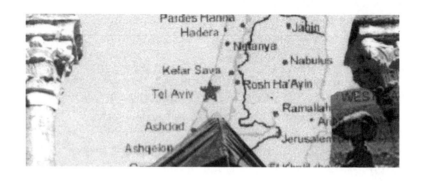

Salman Masalha
Three poems
Translated by Vivian Eden with the author

Born 4 November 1953 in the Arab town of al-Maghar in the
Galilee, Salman Masalha has lived in Jerusalem since 1972. He
studied at the Hebrew University and holds a Ph.D. in classical
Arabic literature, for which he wrote a thesis on mythological
aspects of early Arabic poetry. He taught Arabic language and
literature at the Hebrew University of Jerusalem, and is co-editor
of the *Concordance of Early Arabic Poetry*. He is a bilingual writer
and poet who writes in both Arabic and Hebrew and publishes
translations into both languages. He has published seven
volumes of poetry; his articles, columns, poems and translations
have appeared in newspapers, journals and anthologies in Arabic
and Hebrew as well as in various other languages. He serves on
the editorial board of *Masharef,* an Arabic cultural quarterly. His
last book *Mother Tongue,* was published in 2006. For his Hebrew
book *In Place* (2004) he was awarded the President's Prize for
Hebrew poetry.

If

If one of these days
they were to give me a river
I'd draw my sword
and publicly declare
war on it. If one of these
days they were to give me
ink, I'd sharpen my
pencil and spill the ink
on the sands of the way. I'd
write heretical words in it,
night and day. If they
were to give me endurance
I'd patiently endure
my history with God.
Every time I pray and
beg for His mercy, I
see Him dump in my way
Ten Commandments,
all of them engraved
on banana peels.

(Translated from Arabic by Vivian Eden and Salman Masalha)

In the Dark Room

In the dark room, you see things
you can't see in the lit room.
The alien light that comes from afar
slips into the yard like a shadow
fatigued by the darkness. A black
bird on the windowsill
suckles honey in the fog.
I bear a blessing from the Book
Of Secrets. I reveal the story
of the Vale of Tears. The man
who swam in shallow water
gathers goldfish from
the puddles and protects them
from the thieves for the child
who drowned wetly in a teardrop.
In the dark room you remember
things you had forgotten
in foreign lands. In the darkness
that rises from the longings
for the boy who is not, there is
a back room, filled with a grown
child's memories. Sealed like
a past that never knew a present.
Packed, like a life,
with a surfeit of death.

(Translated from Hebrew by Vivian Eden)

In Praise of Dogs

The white dog, for sure, is useful
for a black day. For instance, if you tell
a dog: Sit, in the tone of a worried person tired by
the pictures piling up on him without shadows,
the dog sits without demur.
Even in a moment of love he might listen, or
gaze at you in admiration.
He understands, without a doubt, that you are still
no professional dog-trainer.
However, a question might remain in the air
as to what happens with an animal
of a different hue.

The black dog understands when you
give him a signal. For instance, if Fate
reverses on you, you just signal to the sitting dog,
and the dog quickly rises towards you.
He recognizes the meanings of gestures when
they wordlessly speak a bit of commiseration.
However, what happens
with another breed of animal?

The spotted dog understands, with canine
intelligence, the kinds of silence. He understands
for instance, the silence of the woe of loss.
There is so much of it now. He understands
the meaning of the silence of illusions for the poet,
and perceives even the silence of death.

However, in this land that keeps loping after
illusions, like a dry river, who dares inquire
what happens with the well-known animals
of the liar species,
like the politicians, and especially
the clerics?

(Translated from Arabic by Vivian Eden and Salman Masalha)

John Berger
Concerning Identity

For thirty years every Palestinian living on Palestinian territory
has been obliged by the Israeli authorities, who illegally occupy
those territories, to carry, at all times, an ID card. Either an
orange one or a green one: orange for those who resided in the
towns under surveillance, and green for those who lived in the
always encircled countryside. Each colour had its own special
restrictions and prohibitions concerning roads, checkpoints, exits
and entrances.

All the information on these Identity Cards was printed in
Hebrew, and only the owner's name was written (by hand) in
Arabic. Name. Photo. Birth date. Birth Place. Residence.

Every card has a number and today when an Israeli soldier taps
in this number on his army mobile telephone, he is informed of
the person's past record. There is scarcely a family in Palestine
who does not have at least one member who has been or is in an
Israeli prison.

Yet despite the stored and coded information, to which these
identity cards are the key, they have nothing to do with identity.
They are simply an inventory of stolen facts.

True identity can be neither delivered on demand nor stored
as mere information. To believe that it can be, is the weakness
of all so-called security records kept by oppressors. True identity

is something known in one heart and recognised within another.
It always contains a secret that no interrogation can reveal. Its
secret is its human-beingness.

And it involves both the personal and the collective. It offers
a sense of belonging and a sense of distinction. (The distinction
being what distinguishes each one of us.) A true identity implies
continuity; it evokes ancestors and heirs, the dead and the as yet
unborn. And, at the same time, it frames a here and now which
is a ME at every transient moment.

The experience of being forced to leave one's homeland, of
being pursued, uprooted and exiled, fractures one's existential
sense of continuity. And this is why the problematic of identity
for the uprooted (the forcibly uprooted) is often linked to the
dream and promise of a return. (The Israelis of all people should
know this but, maintaining that they are the Chosen People,
they have forgotten it.) The four million Palestinians who live
in refugee camps within Palestine and outside, can still know
who they are, and where they belong in history and geography,
because of this promise.

The million Palestinians who reside within the borders of the
state of Israel are officially known as Israeli Arabs. Until recently
the adjective Palestinian was forbidden, and the use of it, under
certain circumstances, was a criminal offence. Today for most
Israeli Jews the very notion of a Palestinian homeland has been
obliterated.

Across the world those who have sophisticated military
superiority, usually have considerable, if not total, control
of the media. And with the help of the media they impose
denigrating stereotypes on those they are oppressing: the
Taliban are primitive fanatics; the Iraqis are uncontrollable
killers. Palestinians are Terrorists (they were Terrorists even
before Al-Qaeda). In addition they are Small-minded, Indolent,
Backward, Obsolete. For the Palestinians themselves such insults
are nothing compared with the real injuries they suffer. But the
idea that the rest of the world may judge Palestinians according
to these monstrous stereotypes, makes their struggle to assert

their true identity harder. And the fact that the outside world fails, time and again, to check Israel's actions – such as the building of the Wall on the West Bank even when those actions have been repeatedly condemned by international law – makes that struggle at times desperate.

Here it's worth reflecting on what recognition – or, let us say, a desirable recognition – of identity involves. It implies accepting the balance between the uniquely personal and the anonymous. Those whom we call the anonymous are not the forgotten, rather they are the nameless who are remembered. Re-membering literally means bringing members together again.

For a people whose identity and land has been annexed and denied for at least three generations, the struggle to preserve and celebrate their identity, takes many forms. There is the intransigence of physical resistance: intransigence in face of the gaping asymmetry of weapons and military means. There are irrepressible popular heroes who, regardless of their political errors, totally embody the denied identity – Arafat is the supreme example. There is poetry which precisely re-members.

> My friends,
> Those left alive among you
> Will let me live another year,
> A year to walk together,
> To fling a river on our backs
> Like gypsies,
> To break the remnants of the structure down
> To bring our tired soul away from its long exile . . .
>   (Mahmoud Darwish, 'Another Year Only')

John Berger

Dvora Amir
Three poems
Translated by Jennie Feldman

Dvora Amir was born in Jerusalem during the 1948 War of Independence. Her parents were from Poland. After the Six-Day War of 1967 she studied Hebrew literature, Jewish philosophy and Kabbala at the Hebrew University of Jerusalem, and in 1975-76, English Literature at the University of Illinois. Today she works at the Centre for Educational Technology in Tel Aviv, where she writes educational programmes on language and literature.

Her first collection *Slow Fire* (1995) received Israel's Kugel Prize for that year. *Documentary Poems* (2003) won the Prime Minister's Award. Her poems have appeared in various literary journals in Israel, and in English translations abroad. Some feature on the website *poetryinternational.org*.

The poems presented here in translation are from *Documentary Poems*, a collection in which the poet relates to her immediate environment and daily life: reminiscences from childhood in divided pre-1967 Jerusalem, memories of lost family members, her travels and poetry reading, and above all, life in a country haunted by terror and the persistent presence of the Occupation. She regards her poems as personal rather than political, offering insights into life in Israel, 'between tragedy and dark hope'.

On the Rim of Abu-Tor

On the rim of Abu-Tor an Arab boy is walking
    across his roof. A schoolbook in his hand,
he goes sure-footed right up to the edge.
    All around is quiet, houses anchored to the slope
like the ships of some giant.
    A brown cow lazing on the path
could be a rusted scrap from a stolen car.
    In front of the house a drainage stream gapes wide
moistens its throat as if waiting for its prey.
    Why do his confident steps cast such terror upon me?
Something intimately foreign creeping
    through me like the vine that weaves
entwined between our courtyards.
    He walks, and I dare not take my eyes off him,
as if my gazing were bidden to protect his soul.
    I tend to the flowers in my plot, I water them
but my heart is on watch for his every step
    dangling like my life before my eyes.

(A*bu-Tor is a mixed Jewish-Arab neighbourhood on the south-eastern edge
    of Jerusalem.*)

'The Seam'

The Seam isn't invisibly stitched, hidden away in my life.
It is woven into my body, branded within me like a tattoo.
A nursery school in Mamilla, a bombed-out building by the
    city wall,
Upper steps hanging in emptiness, nowhere to hold,
Leading down to a darkened pit and in its depths
A writhing viper – the line of the seam.
When you touch it you suddenly slither into the Valley of
    Ben Hinnom,
Into the gaping maw of the demon of hell
As he came from the lanes of Beit Tannus
To gorge on fresh children
Every morning, every morning.

('The Seam' [Heb. Kav ha-tefer] was the 1948-67 armistice line
separating Jerusalem's Jordanian- and Israeli-controlled sectors. It
was a zone of recurrent hostilities. Like the Mamilla neighbourhood,
the Valley of Ben Hinnom [Heb. Gai ben-Hinnom, or Gehenom,
'hell'] lay along the Seam. Mentioned several times in the Bible, it was
notorious as the site of child sacrifices to the Canaanite god Moloch.)

War Games

After 1948 we moved to the West Nicoforia neighbourhood
not far from the Franciscans' Pontifical Institute.
The street was named after Wauchope, British High
    Commissioner.
We played war. On the stair landings
we set up a field hospital,
each step was a bed for casualties from the fighting.
The girls were tender-hearted nurses, the boys medics.
The mortally wounded we put on the topmost landing.
Activity there was frantic during emergencies.
We hung plastic bags for infusions,
we changed bandages, gave on-the-spot first aid,
stabilized the wounded case by case, gave transfusions.
There were sighs of grief, cries of agony from the wounded.
One of the neighbours, a nasty man, always trod on our
    patients,
the others were mostly considerate, seeing the difficult
    situation
and tiptoed past on the edge of the stairs.
Conditions were awful. To clear a passage
we of course had to ask the wounded to scrunch up their legs.
Our emergency room was the mail-box area.
The wonders we worked there, saving the mortally stricken.
We tended everyone, regardless, with infinite dedication,
though sometimes our efforts failed.
And already we knew phrases like 'fell into a coma', 'departed
    this life'.
Then we'd hold our valedictory ritual,
for we knew how to pay our last respects,
for we knew what war is about.

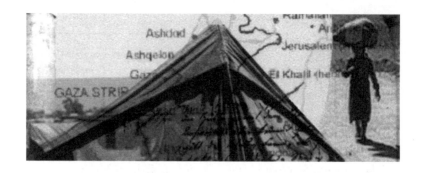

Jennie Feldman

Sage Tea

*. . .they shall sit every man under his vine and under his fig tree;
and none shall make them afraid.* Micah 4:4

I

His season isn't ours.
Not with mottled vine leaves
clenched for the letting go
any moment now
and memory hankering for
those globes' sweetness, as if
we'd dreamt the mistimed pruning,
the sap we couldn't staunch
welling, dropping to earth
like suicide.

II
No sheltering fig leaves either.

Not with a single sapling
knee-high all these years and thus
beyond the pale of scripture

like the pungent sage next to it,
the vintage answer in these parts
to fright or a nervous cough.

Autumn 2003

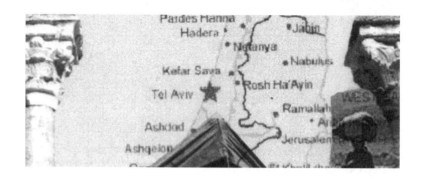

Ghassan Zaqtan
'Alone and the river before me'
Translated by Fady Joudah

Ghassan Zaqtan (b. 1954) is a Palestinian living in Ramallah. A prominent poet, he has also written two novels, a play, and two scripts for documentary film. His work has been translated into French, Italian, and Norwegian among other languages.

Alone and the river before me

I have a suspicious heart, brother,
and a blind statue,
and the news that amateur refugees brought from Baghdad
  stunned me
there's a lot they haven't seen yet
they were crossing the bridge by chance

intentions are in the ports
befuddled as their owners left them,
incomplete as the murdered left them
and where our friend, the one you know, pointed, we went
without a moan or groan

our country is far
and intentions good

we left, as exiles leave, houses more beautiful than the roads
and women more faithful than passers-by
we weren't discouraged and our will wasn't stolen

we dreamt, as residents dream, of roads more beautiful than
    the houses
of women who furnished our bodies and altered our language
though this took us neither to hill nor sea

an infantry marching out of some front appeared
we heard its drone but didn't see it, and with worn-out eyes
and cracked feet they shook off the mud over the marble
and dried their boots on the billboards of the 'founding
    father'

we watched
as if we had seen nothing, heard nothing

and it was possible to remember their lustful dreams, chase
    the ghosts
and touch the buttocks of women to be sure it was just a
    dream!

but there's no mercy for the dead in these cold corners
no reward for those who are in the know

there's only listening to the mountain where caves are born
and darkness grows like a carnivorous plant . . .

the cry of the birds at the bursting dawn didn't overtake us
we didn't stumble over the wisdom or obsessions of our
    predecessors
though what we saw is worth telling!

. . . and then
a bunch of slaves started climbing out of a hole, up the walls
even if the doors were wide open
they climbed down to the city, roamed its markets
men and children were shouting in the dark
swatting it with drums and dancing,
women undressing on the edge of an abyss to distract death
from their children
as one of the locals explained to us

we felt grateful for our exile and residence

and said to ourselves:
we are only marching exiles, our shadows don't trail us over
    the earth
and like textile workers we hold threads and spin them to
    weave memories
that breathe behind us and follow our steps like bewildered
    dogs

who are we that we should dislike what we don't know
or love what we have no business in!

then a jealous boy appeared:
his jealousy remained glistening on the fence after he left
and it blocked the path of cats, pedestrians, and the scent of
    basil
after the amateur refugees, with the news from Baghdad, had
    gone

his jealousy leaned on the breasts of a young woman
who came out of the shadows and took off her veil, placed it
on the grass by the soldiers' boots
just as I was moving to another dream . . .

all this would have been worthy of consideration and
    repetition
had a young philosopher from Ramallah not died at 4:16 that
    morning
surrounded by his students, admirers, and three friends
(two men and a woman) it would have been possible also to
    remember
and add other scattered things
so grief can appear and treason mature

chief among them
Buddha's lilac statue

or the photograph of a house owner in his furnished living
    room
staring at us out of his conservative classical death

the father's hermetic contemplation
a complicity of sorts with the daughter
as he expires beneath the oxygen apparatus

a woman's voice as she conceals her infidelity
through the phone's ten thick layers

it would have been possible to document his death or to
    remember
other scattered things in another context, like his dead
    weight
or the white of his eyes resembling a final resurrection
before the sirens were lit

if only he did not stand a bit crooked from the world, as
    happened with Cavafy
whose poetry he did not concern himself with as he did other
    poets

I have a suspicious heart, brother
and my stance is whole
there is no one who can guess the whirling in my head
and I no longer trust those night travellers!

&&&

I have a suspicious heart and my admirers are obstinate
and in the wadis
if you look closely are birds and hunters
who wear in the dark longing's smell
and its form

hunters who have other motives in the light
other labyrinths
and paths that make a hyena pant
and the signifier and the signified are lost

among them:
wind-instrument blowers

wily attars in the markets

barefoot narrators behind the slaves

and pretentious mockers standing on their bank
where we were born
white from black fathers

there are among them more than enough to make me
    superfluous . . .

my guests are blind and dervishes
as aforementioned
I describe them as they appeared
in secret
as blessed and guarded narrators born
with absent minds
but if absently
they died they'd notice

in meaning they have a jinn's rank
and its language
and in structure a paranoid's body
and levity

. . . and for some reason I can't quite recall now
he moved a little away, turned his back to me and stared at
    the river
and said: I have nothing left to give you except this:
and pointed to the water
then wiped my face with his hands

I became alert and imagined I was in a garden in Baghdad
    whose fence
I had passed by when I was a kid . . .
and there was in the dark a fishing boat
a soft paddle transmitting the scent of sparks from across the
    river
quiet sounds coming from the brothel,
and all this seemed to me like breathing . . .
what I don't see as it has gathered

I rose and looked around
and there I was alone and the river before me,
with two maidens in it, one black, the other white
and whenever I slept or was distracted he would come, sit
    before me,
talk to me and I would listen, then he'd wipe his hands
with my face and I'd awaken, transported from one land to
    another land
one time to another time...

until I reached the Tigris bank that night where the two
    maidens were
and I realized the state I had been in, and longed for those
    I'd left behind

so I composed these lines for the occasion:

I raise your secret to all	expose mine to man and jinn
I light a fire of jasmine	and chase a dream of fleeing mirth
I gather behind you the crowd's shadow	a salaam of vanishing to the vanished
and in pleasure I am alluring	and in sleep I see the invisible
as if I were your radiance	and you my whirling spell
I played and spun the soul of life	as one seeks a plaything
and let loose prophetic horses	and rode drunker than a drunk
so here I am before you	a triumph brought to the victor
you're all I have as I'm paraded	the pleased around his benefactor

I elevated him higher in my prayers and embellished his
    favours then remembered
what he had told me as he was bidding me farewell:

'as for that which you did not ask me about
it's your secret, no one else's
and it doesn't concern me
I neither help you with it
nor release you from it'

and I had asked him about all things but this!

he had tutored me
when I was a kid,
I would repeat whatever he said
three times
before the rooster crowed,
I would listen
then repeat what he had said twice
and by the third time
I'd add to it my own.

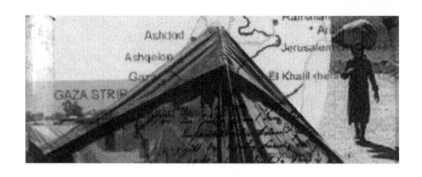

Tal Nitzan
Three poems
Translated by the author with Vivian Eden

The target

They closed their non-aiming eye
and watched the target
and chose an aiming point
and brought the edge of the blade
to the notch of the rear sight
with all the gunsights upright
and leaving a white thread
they shot.
But missed.
Managed to kill Muhamad El-Hayk, 24,
and severely wound his father Abdalla, 64,
all 'as needed and according to procedures',
but missed Maisun El-Hayk,
only slightly wounded her
in spite of her big belly

that happened to be a perfect aiming point
(but hadn't they made her undress at the roadblock before
to ensure the belly was a belly indeed
and the labour pains – labour pains
before it occurred to them
to proceed with
'suspect arrest procedure'?)
and also failed to hit
her foetus daughter
and send her to heaven
before she came to this world
– must have overlooked that white thread –
but did manage to inseparably seam
her birth day to her father's burial
and reinforce the promise
'in sorrow thou shalt bring forth children'
– no greater sorrow has been! –
as the shooting ceased
and Maisun called out for Muhamad
and the terror or the excruciating pain
twisted her voice
('Breathe slowly and deeply,
find the most comfy position,
think of something nice and pleasant,
ask your partner to dim the lights,
play your favourite music,
gently massage your lower back')
and he, suddenly, stopped answering,
for if you haven't seen Maisun's photo,
her hands quivering over her daughter,
pink, calm, innocent
the way newborn babes are
– however, she was lucky
to have given birth to her on the hospital bed
rather than crouch like her sisters before her
like an animal in front of the soldiers

and then stumble ten kilometers,
walking and bleeding,
carrying the dead infant as an offering –
if you haven't opened a non-aiming eye
to look at Maisun El-Hayk's face,
you've never seen
bringing children forth in sorrow.

Night

The humming of a benign machine.
Our clothes our dishes or our words roll inside it.

The slight child will be heavy with sleep
as she is carried from bed to bed.
A book will be slipped from the grip of her hand.

This is when my body splits into countless foes
in the cat's eyes.
If I scold it strikes. If I don't it strikes.

Another man was shot today before he made it home.
The house plants shrug their leaves in renunciation, or regret:

'From now on you are on your own.'

Cover

At night I bend over good and bad children alike, sharing a sleep in
which they are mine.
Fernando Pessoa, *The Book of Disquiet*

At this dark hour
all children are alike.
At this darkness the very word 'children'
is enough to make you cringe with dread
The truck's mouth opens, Salima Matria
looks for treasures in the dump,
soon he will be covered by the garbage mound
Cover, the hand reaches for the blankets
that swell over their innocence,
the blankets that haven't even fallen off
Ahmed Zar'una will not climb again
on the big armoured toy,
his heart flutters in his thin chest
inside the rifle's sight
Thus, fists over head,
love is tied to nightmare.

(*Translated by Tal Nitzan*)

Vivian Eden
From Arabic to Hebrew and Hebrew to Arabic: Poetry Translation as a Microcosm of How the World Ought to Work

It is a fact rarely acknowledged that 20 per cent of Israel's citizens are Palestinian Arabs. This applies both inside Israel and in international cultural and political circles – Arab, Jewish and neither.

One rare acknowledgement came in the years 2001 to 2005. The Helicon Society for the Advancement of Poetry in Israel held joint residential Arabic-Hebrew workshops for poets at the outset of their careers once a month over a period of six months with about sixteen participants in each group, selected on the basis of merit from hundreds of applicants. Among the topics addressed each weekend were principles of poetry translation, with exercises mostly in the translation of English poetry into both languages and collaborative inter-translation – the translation of the participants' works from Arabic into Hebrew and from Hebrew into Arabic.

It has long been evident why it is good for any poet to translate poems from other languages:

Translation is good reading followed by good writing.

The first stage in translating a poem – careful reading – means identifying and understanding the discrete elements of a poem and comprehending how they all work together. This is excellent practice for identifying issues in one's own work, yet devoid of all the ego problems and blind spots one encounters as a novice in criticizing and polishing one's own work. As Frank MacShane, who pioneered the literary translation seminar at Columbia University, put it, 'translation may be useful to a writer in developing his own literary skills. He can concentrate on problems of expression without becoming emotionally involved in the work's structural and thematic problems, since in one way or another, they have already been solved by the author of the original.'

Anyone who has ever translated a poem knows that it is nearly impossible to reproduce the whole of the original in the target language, and anyone who has ever written a poem knows that you can't get every aspect of the trigger experience or insight into the poem and you need to choose those elements that are most important, striking and effective. Anyone who works with beginning writers is aware of the difficulty of persuading them to leave anything out. Translation teaches discipline, pruning, the justification of choices and letting go, even of things that are held dear.

Translating in a group, particularly a culturally mixed group, is also excellent for developing the ability to formulate and accept constructive criticism and to seek agreed solutions to problems. If only these lessons could be learned in political contexts too.

The second stage in a translation is writing the poem in the target language. Here, the issue of responsible choice is foregrounded:

Translation calls attention to the mechanics of the target language – the writer's own language – and to assumptions of both the source and the target cultures.

An English-speaker, unless called upon to do so in a classroom situation, will not pause to consider the difference between 'I was walking' and 'I walked' but will simply make the right choice in his speech or writing. However, confronted with the necessity of translating, for example, an English sentence like 'Marc Antony was walking down Fifth Avenue when Bob Dylan walked right past him', a Hebrew-speaker will have to deal with the fact that the verb in his language does not make a distinction between a completed action in the past – walked – and a continuous action in the past – was walking. The translator might therefore have to add elements to the sentence to make the narrative situation clear, and might also pause to consider the greater implications inherent in the grammar of English, and absent in the grammar of the Hebrew, of the possibility of expressing the slicing of the past in more than one way – which is not a minor issue at all in the politics of the country we share.

Another sort of problem is encapsulated in 'Fifth Avenue'. I could easily translate the word for 'fifth' and the word for 'avenue' into Hebrew, say – *hashdera hahamishit* – but by doing this, I will lose something of the universally-known glamour of that particular street in New York. Alternatively, I could transliterate the words 'Fifth Avenue' but then it would come out sounding awkwardly and provincially like *feeft evenyu* in Hebrew or *fiffith awenyu* in Arabic. Suddenly I realize that my language has fewer vowel sounds than English, and a rather different set of consonant sounds. I need to choose whether to translate or to transliterate the place name, and I also need to decide whether I will make it my invariable practice to follow the same rule for, say, the Champs Elysées and Unter den Linden, or decide on a case-by-case basis. Place names are particularly fraught. For example, I live in Jerusalem in English and *Yerushalaiyim* in Hebrew, but in Arabic is it *Urshalim* or *Al Quds* – which is far more laden with religious and cultural meanings? Or is it the clumsy Israel Broadcasting Authority Arabic service compromise: *Urshalim al Quds?*

Translation means reading other literatures, which leads to the enrichment of both individuals and cultures.

This is hardly an interesting observation. However, in a situation like the one that prevails between writers of Hebrew and writers of Arabic, it is exceedingly important, particularly for the writers of Hebrew who, unless they specialize in Arabic studies in secondary school and university, are not exposed at all to Arabic poetry or for that matter Muslim and Christian Scripture. By contrast, in the Arab-language schools in Israel, some modern Hebrew literature, as well as Old Testament and Talmud are taught. This asymmetry in knowledge was a source of dismay to the Hebrew-speakers and a source of ironic pride to the Arabic speakers.

Reading poetry in the other's language also draws attention to what is universal. One writer of Hebrew, a business administration student, told a reporter about his experience working on the translation of a poem of his couched as a letter from a mother on the anniversary of her son's death: 'For Jews, most of the bereavement for mothers is a result of the encounter with Arabs. There I was sitting with an Arab woman, translating the poem. I felt that my context was foreign to her, but the feelings I expressed were universal. Politically, you can be on either side, but every mother loves her boy.' An Arab lawyer and poet from the northern town of Tira commented: 'Translation is no simple matter. It is like creating something anew. It involves a kind of intimacy with the poet. You get to know him, enter his private places and emotions, and come to an understanding of how he sees things.'

Translation in a group teaches that translators, like poets, have individual voices and that there is more than one good solution to every problem.

Israel's Hebrew-speaking population is for the most part a population of immigrants and children of immigrants. This accounts in part for the fact that literary translation has always been a part of the culture; the comparison of translations is almost a national pastime. In training writers, seeing and hearing a number of translations enables the hearing of distinct voices. It is impossible to have everyone write the same poem, but it is possible to have everyone translate the same poem. This makes it possible to clarify the understanding of each poet-translator's unique translating voice, which, as we have found is very like his or her own unique poetic voice. Learning to translate is learning to listen to others and to ourselves.

Where language groups exist uneasily side by side, translating poetry leads to better understanding, the dispelling of misunderstandings and a justified sense of mutual accomplishment.

Inter-translation worked like this: Since all of the writers of Arabic could read Hebrew but very few of the writers of Hebrew could read Arabic, the writers of Arabic were asked to make a transliteration into Hebrew or Latin letters of one of their poems, so that in addition to hearing it read aloud everyone could also 'see' what the poem sounds like – repetition, rhyme, alliteration and so on. Writers of both languages were asked to prepare a line-by-line 'kit', calling attention to intertextualities and customs that are culture-bound, for example: 'We always serve only water and unsweetened black coffee to people who come to console mourners'; 'This word *tashlih* literally means "something thrown" but it is ordinarily used only to refer to the custom of symbolically casting out one's sins from one's pockets into a body of water on the second day of Rosh Hashanah and the prayer that is said then.'

Pairs or small groups of speakers of the respective languages work together on a literal translation of the poem from one language to the other – Hebrew to Arabic or Arabic to Hebrew – all the while explaining and asking questions about the text. For example: 'This is a reference to a verse in the Koran – let's look it up'; 'In your language you have two different words for earning your own living and for making money to support your family. In our language, we use the same word for both. What can we do about that?' Once this process is completed a speaker or a pair of speakers of the target language make a polished translation.

As a method of verification, someone who spoke both of the languages, but was not in the group that worked on the particular translation, took the translation and rendered it back into the source language – a practice that proved very illuminating and helpful in catching nuances and misunderstandings before the final polishing of the translation.

We always came out of the sessions with the feeling that this is the way the world ought to work. Perhaps this activity could also be developed in other places where language groups exist uneasily side by side, as for example within the expanded European Union along the German-Polish border or in the states of former Yugoslavia.

Acknowledgements
*The system for inter-translation was developed over the years along with my colleagues, especially Helicon director Amir Or, based on methods used by Professor Daniel Weissbort at the Translation Workshop of the International Writers' Program and the Department of Comparative Literature at the University of Iowa, by Martin Mooij at Poetry International in Rotterdam and by **Poetry Ireland**, which has an extensive program of translation by poets. A more extensive description of the practice may be found (in German) in: Vivian Eden, 'Über Sinn und Möglichkeiten der lyrischen Übersetzung in der Schreibschule' in **Schreiben lernen Schreiben lehren**, Frankfurt am Main, 2006.*

Yosef Sharon
'The Shelter'
Translated by Gabriel Levin

Yosef Sharon lives in Tel Aviv and has published since the seventies four collections of poetry, the most recent, *The Inheritors,* in 1998. He has taught a graduate workshop in literary criticism at Haifa University. He is also an essayist and writer of short prose, notably *Saturday Morning,* a text accompanying a collection of photographs taken at the turning of the millennium by the photographer Simcha Shirman.

The Shelter

A stack of my father's old, worm-eaten books
were moved to the shelter after being treated for mildew,
all the perforated knowledge of diligent
scholars hidden from the human eye – research on disputes
between workers and their employers, conflicts
which are now called by other names, crouch like the
    ostracized

in a rigid carton, stiff-backed,
as though deluding themselves that their future
still lies before them, as though only terminologies change,
and accordingly nothing becomes dated,
and the authors appear to be waiting soberly for the results,
the foreseeable struggle
and its aftermath in the suffocating space – eighteen
years after the demise of the books' owner.
Stashed below, to save the 'spotless' books above, on the top
    floor.
No one touched the books for a year, but that year
a storm lantern warmed Arab day-labourers,
and they wrote to its light
on a chart outlined on the wall
Hebrew words in Arabic transcription (without grasping their
    meaning?)
Hebrew names transcribed in Arabic,
as something marginal to their present lives,
a gag between meals wolfed down before the curfew,
swallowing Hebrew on their lips without learning it, without
    scorn.
And they refused to leave a trace of suffering –
neither a wounded gazelle, nor a slaughtered hare.
There are no adjectives.
They only stretch out their hands, unknowingly,
warming themselves by the lantern's flame.

(Note: In the mid-nineties, Palestinians from the West Bank and Gaza
would enter Israel in the early hours of the morning to scrape a living
in a variety of menial day jobs. Movement in and out of the territories,
however, was frequently restricted by curfews imposed by the military.)

Mahmoud Darwish
'Like a Hand Tattoo in the Jahili Poet's Ode'
Translated by Fady Joudah

Mahmoud Darwish is among the two or three most important
poets writing in Arabic today. 'Like a Hand Tattoo' is the third
long poem in a quartet under the heading of *Exile* in Darwish's
latest collection, *Like Almond Blossoms or Farther.* The four poems
employ dialogue between the self and its various others, where
the wayward lyricist and the playwright meet. Here the 'other' is
a ghost, a relic of the self. 'Hand Tattoo', summons the opening
line of the pre-Islamic (*Jahili*) poet Tarfah Ibn el-Abd's *mu'allaqah*,
where the ruins of home are 'like the remnants of a tattoo on the
back of the hand'. Thus Darwish's poem engages the ancient,
rich tradition of Arabic poetry, its fundamental sense of exile,
with its contemporary aesthetic. Also, the structure of the poem,
its circularity perhaps, pays tribute to the practice of the Sufi
Arab poet, as he flies 'in the words...to anywhere'. Darwish is the
recipient of several international literary awards. His latest book
in English collects three full-length volumes in *The Butterfly's
Burden*, from Bloodaxe.

Like a Hand Tattoo in the Jahili Poet's Ode

I am he, he walks ahead of me and I follow him.
I don't say to him: Right here, right here, a simple thing was
     ours:
Green stone. Trees. A street. A youthful moon. A reality
no more. He walks ahead of me, and I walk on his shadow in
     pursuit . . .
whenever he speeds up, shadow rises over the hills,
covers a pine tree in the south, and a willow in the north:
Haven't we already parted? I asked. He said: Indeed!
I offered you imagination's return to the real
and you offered me the apple of gravity.
I said: Where are you taking me then?
He said: Towards the beginning, where you were born,
right here, you and your name.

If it were up to me to bring back the beginning I would
have chosen for my name fewer letters,
easier letters on the foreign woman's ears. March
is the month of storms and emotional yearning.
Spring blooms like a whim in a chat between two,
before a lengthy summer and after a long winter. I remember
only metaphor. I had been barely born
when I noticed a clear resemblance between
the horse's mane and my mother's braids.

Drop metaphor, and take a stroll on the woolly earth, he said.

Sunset brings the stranger back to his well, like a song
that isn't sung, and sunset kindles in us
a longing for a mysterious desire.

Perhaps, perhaps, I said. Everything is an analysis
at sunset. And memories might awaken a calling
that resembles the gesture of death at sunset
or the cadence of a song that isn't sung to anyone:

> Over cypress trees
> east of passion
> there are gilded clouds
> and in the heart a chestnut
> dark-skinned beauty
> diaphanous in shadow
> I drink her like water
> It's time we frolic
> time we travel
> to any planet.

I am he, he walks upon me, and I ask him:
Do you remember anything here?
If you do, ease your tread upon me
because the earth is pregnant with us.

He says: I have seen here in the prairie a bright moon
with a brilliant sorrow like an orange at night
guiding us to the road of wandering.
Without it, mothers wouldn't have found their children.
Without it, the night travellers wouldn't have read
their names suddenly upon the night: 'Refugees'
guests of the wind.

My wings were still small for the wind that year . . .
I used to think place was known
by the mothers and the scent of sage. No one
told me this place is called a country
and that behind the country there were borders, and behind
the borders a place called wandering and exile
for us. I wasn't yet in need of identity . . .

but those who reached us aboard
their combat tanks were transferring the place
swiftly away

     Place is the passion.

Those are our relics, like a hand tattoo
in the Jahili poet's ode, they pass through us
and we through them – he, the one I once was, said to me
when I didn't know enough words to know the names of our
    trees
or to call the birds that gather in me by their names.
I wasn't able to memorize the words and protect the place
from being transferred to a strange name fenced in
with eucalyptus trees. While the posters told us:
'You were never here.'

    Yet the storm softens
    and place is the passion.

Those are our relics, the one I once was said . . .
Right here two epochs meet then part, so who are you
in the company of the present?
I said: Had it not been for the smoke of factories,
I would have said: I am you.
He said: And who are you in yesterday's presence?
I said: Had it not been for the meddling
of the present tense, I would have said: I am we.
He said: And in tomorrow's presence?

I said: I am a love poem you will write when you
yourself choose the myth of love:

    Her skin is wheat colour like old harvest songs
    she's dark from the sting of the night,
    white from so much laughing water

when she approached the spring . . .
Her eyes are two almonds
and two wounds of honey are her lips

Her legs are marble towers
and on my shoulders her hands are flying birds
I have a soul she gave me
a soul fluttering around the place.

Drop metaphor, and walk with me! he said! Do you see
a trace of the butterfly in the light?
I said: I see you there, I see you passing
like an ancestral notion.
He said: That's how the butterfly recovers
her poetic tasks: a song the astronomers
inscribe only as evidence of eternity's rightness.

Easily I walk upon myself and my shadow
follows. Nothing brings me back
and nothing brings him back,
as if I were someone of me bidding me farewell
in a hurry for his tomorrow.
He tells me: Wait for no one, not even for me.
And I don't bid him farewell.

And it seems like poetry: over the hill
a cloud deceives me, knits its identity around me
and bequeaths me an orbit I never lose.

Place has its scent
sunset has its agonies
the gazelle has its hunter
the turtles have their armour
for self-defence
the ants have a kingdom
the birds have their trysts

the horses their names
the wheat its feast
and as for anthem, the anthem of happy finale
has no poet.

In the last fraction of life we listen only
to our aching joints or to a mosquito droning
like a philosopher who wakes us from sleep.
In the last fraction, we sense the pain
of two amputated legs, as if the feeling reached us late.
We didn't notice our inner wound when we were young,
a wound like an oil-painting of a fire that blazes the colours
of our flag and kindles the bull of our anthem.
In the last fraction of life dawn bursts
only because the kindhearted angels
are coerced to perform their tasks . . .

I am he, my self's coachman,
no horse whinnies in my language.

He said: We'll walk even if it is the last fraction
of life, even if the paths let us down.
We'll fly, as a Sufi does, in the words . . . to anywhere.

On a hill high as two heavenly hands we rose
and walked on thorns and holm oak needles,
we blanketed ourselves with the wool of orphaned plants,
united with the dictionary of our names.
I said: Do you feel the poke
of pebbles and the cunning of sand grouse?
He said: I don't feel a thing!
As if feeling is a luxury, as if I am
one adjective of the many absence has.
My life is not with me, it has left me as a woman
leaves a spectre-man, she waited
but got bored with waiting, so she guided another

to her feminine treasure . . . if there must be a moon
let it be full, and not a banana horn

I said: You will need some time to know yourself,
so sit on a partition, in-between,
because the how is no longer how, and the where is not a
    where . . .

On two heavenly rocks we waited for the sunset
of the gazelle. At sunset the stranger feels
his need to embrace another stranger, at sunset
the two strangers feel a third in their midst: one
who interferes in what they might or might not say . . .

> The two of you should bid what was
> and what will be farewell.
> Farewell to the nūn in rhyme
> in the dual name
> and in the indigo land!

I said: Who is he?
But an echo answered from afar: I am the realistic one here.
The voice of your destinies. A bulldozer
driver who changed the spontaneity of this place
and cut the braids of your olive trees to match
the soldiers' hair and open a path for the mule

of an ancient prophet. I am the realistic, the tamer of myth.

He is the third of two who sit on two heavenly rocks,
but he doesn't see us as we are:
An old man with a child under his wing, and a child
enmeshed in the old man's wisdom.

We said: Salaam unto man and jinn around us.
He said: I don't get the metaphor.

We said: Why have you infiltrated what we say and what we
   sense?
He said: The way your shadow wears pebbles
and sand grouse startled me.
We asked: What are you afraid of?
He said: The shadow . . . at times it has the scent of garlic,
other times the scent of blood.
- From where did you come?
- From non place. For every place
far from God or his land is exile. Who are you?
- We are the grandchildren of the soul of this place.
We were born here, and here we will live if the Lord remains
   alive.
And every place far from God or his land is exile.
- The way your shadow wears the place raises suspicion.
- What do you suspect?
- A shadow struggling with another shadow?
- Is it because the distance between yesterday
and our present remains fertile for the trinity of time?
- It was yesterday that I killed you.
- Death pardoned us.
- I am eternity's watchman, he shouted:

> Say farewell to what was
> and what will be
> say farewell to the scent of garlic
> and blood in the shadow of this place . . .

But what's the meaning of this thing,
this thing that makes me
a self then gives back to meaning its features?
How am I born from a thing I later make?

I extend in the high trees and the thing raises me
to heaven, I become a cautious bird
that nothing deceives or obliterates.

In each thing I see my soul, and what I cannot feel hurts me.
And what doesn't feel the hurt my soul causes it also hurts
   me.
I and I don't believe in this dirt road yet we walk trailing the
   ant line
(tracking is the map of instinct). And neither the sun has
completely set, nor has the orange moon become fully lit.

I and I don't believe the beginning
waits for those who return to it, like a mother on the house's
   doorstep.
Yet we walk even if the sky fails us.

I and I don't believe the story
brought us back as two witnesses to what we had done:
I forgot about you like my cherry stained shirt
when I ran into a forest and became filled with regret . . .
And I, too, forgot about you when I kept for myself a phoenix
feather, and became filled with regret.

Shall we make amends then? I asked him.
He said: Hold on. There, two metres away from us,
is my school, let's go and rescue the alphabet
from the spider web, though we'll leave for it the weeping
   vowels!
I remember it, I said: Two ancient walls without a ceiling
like two letters of a language distorted by sand
and by a Sodom-like earthquake. Fat cows sleeping over the
   alphabet.
A dog wagging the tail of mirth and content. And a small
   night
readying its things for the bustle of foxes.
He said: Life always continues its custom after us.
What a thing! What a shameless thing life is, it only thinks
of fulfilling its desires.
I said: Shall we make amends then and share

this absence. We are here alone in the poem?
He said: Hold on. There, on the edge of the hill,
on the east side, lies the family's graveyard.
Let's go before the dark descends over the dead
and bid salaam unto the sleeping,
those who dream of their paradise garden
safe and sound, salaam unto the lightly ascending
on the ladder of God.

In the presence of death we grasp only the accuracy of our
    names . . .
A lewd absurdity. We found not one stone
that carries a victim's name, not my name or yours.
Which of the two of us died, I asked, me or I?

He said: I don't know anymore.
I said: Shall we make amends?
He said: Hold on!
I said: Is this the return we have always desired?
He said: A comedy by one of our frivolous goddesses.
Have you enjoyed the visit thus far?
I said: Is this the end of your exile?
He said: And the beginning of yours.
I said: What's the difference?
He said: The cunning of eloquence.
I said: Eloquence isn't necessary for defeat.
He said: Yes it is. Eloquence convinces a widow
to marry a foreign tourist, eloquence protects
the roses of the garden from the frivolity of the wind.
- Then let's make amends?
- If the dead and the living sign, in one body, a truce.
- Here I am, the dead and the living.
- I forgot you, who are you?
- I am your 'I', its duplicate, your 'I' that noticed what
the butterfly said to me: O my brother in fragility...
He said: But the butterfly has already burned.
- Then don't burn as it has.

And I turned toward him, but didn't see him, so I screamed
with all my strength: Wait, wait for me! Take everything
from me except my name.

He didn't wait for me, he flew away . . .
Then the night reached me, and my shout drew
a spectre passing by.

I said: Who are you?
He said: Salaam unto you. I said: And unto you,
who are you?

He said: I am a foreign tourist who loves your myths.
And I would love to marry one of Anat's widowed daughters!

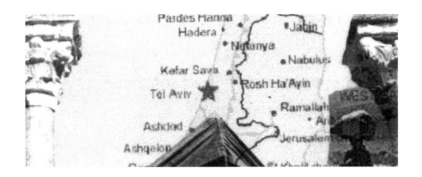

Rivka Miriam
Four poems
Translated by Linda Zisquit

Rivka Miriam was born in 1952 in Jerusalem, where she continues to live and work. Daughter of the renowned Yiddish writer Leib Rochman and named for his mother and sister who perished in the Holocaust, Rivka Miriam's first poetry collection was published in 1966, when she was fourteen. She has published twelve books of poetry, two collections of short stories and two books for children, and has received numerous literary awards. Rivka Miriam has twice been the recipient of the Prime Minister's Award; she has also received the Goldberg Prize and the Holon Prize, both distinguished awards for Hebrew literature. Her books include *Tree Touches Tree* (1978), *The Sounds Towards Them* (1982), *From Poems of Stone Mothers* (1988), *Place, Tiger* (1994) *Nearby Was the East* (1996), *Resting Jew* (2000) *Said the Investigator* (2005), *Miracle Owner, and Other Passers-by* (2006), and *My Father Commanded Me Not to Die* (2007). Also a painter whose work was first shown at the Tel Aviv Museum when she was sixteen, Rivka Miriam has worked for many years as head of Beit Midrash *Elul*, an important Jerusalem Jewish Studies centre. *These Mountains: Selected Poems of Rivka Miriam*, translated by Linda Zisquit will be published in a bi-lingual edition this year.

During this entire period someone
looks at us from the hills

And during this entire period someone looks at us from the
    hills
his voice is not heard, but his lips move
and we do not know if he is cursing, or if he is blessing
and when I see him
like the ticking of a clock, the pulse beats in my thigh.

And still that someone looks at us
from the hills

And still that someone looks at us from the hills.
And still his voice is not heard, but his lips indeed move.
And we do not know if there, on his guard, he's fallen asleep,
    or if he's still awake
and there is no sign and no signal – and no clue to what is
    coming
if he will make us inherit serenity – or if he will anger
and from his bitter anger we will all be shaken –

to that someone I send
caressing fingers
and as a lightning rod I pull –

what is pulled is only a transparent echo coming from the
    hills.

The poems here are about our family

The poems here are about our family, the one whose borders
    are unknown
about our tribe, small, expanded
our tribe, which, like sand, death does not govern
and which, after its death, shines like a star.
Here among us is Joseph naked of his coat. Here are his
    brothers, too.
And the folded pit which was carried on Joseph's back. And
    the yearning woman with whom he did not sleep.
The poems that are inscribed here are also written about me.
    Me, about whom no one knows
from where I came
and no one knows to where I will go.
And about our God, who reveals himself or hides, in order to
    hide that he still reigns.
And about the belly. The one, round, which is all
    pleasantness
this belly, which the land itself looks into,
to research its seasons
to know its secret.
And about our fear which lives in the yard as a loyal little
    dog joyful and barking,
if only we would scratch behind its ear, it would lie down
    pampered.
Also about the terrible pain that does not cease.
And about the gate which has no one to open
about this body which covers itself with a sheet, sometimes
    out of grace, sometimes out of doom.

And in the inner room we guard the heaviness of the mouth

And in the inner room we guard Moses' heavy mouth
Isaac's weak eyes, Jacob's dragged leg.
And when war comes upon us, into the inner room we enter
to watch them from up close.
For each one who goes out to battle, only with these will he
    wrap himself.

Samih al-Qasim
Four poems
Translated by Nazih Kassis

One of the foremost Palestinian poets and a major figure in the Arab world, Samih al-Qasim was born in 1939, in Zarqa, Jordan, to a Palestinian Druze family from the Galilee. He grew up in the village of Rama and experienced the Palestinian tragedy of 1948 first hand, achieving fame as one of the celebrated 'resistance poets' during the 1950s. His first book was published when he was just eighteen, and over the decades he has produced a body of work that is as varied and innovative as it is large. He has also written novels, plays, and numerous essays, and has worked for years as an editor and journalist. Today a citizen of Israel and still a resident of Rama, Samih al-Qasim is an outspoken opponent of racism and oppression on all sides of the Middle East conflict. His first English collection, *Sadder Than Water*, was published recently by Ibis Editions in Jerusalem; the book (translated by Nazih Kassis) collects poems from his various periods and modes and presents readers with the full range of al-Qasim's oeuvre, which is characterized by its ironic approach to painfully charged political situations, its melancholy music, and its lyrical evocation of Palestinian heritage.

End of Talk with a Jailer

From the narrow window of my small cell,
I see trees that are smiling at me
and rooftops crowded with my family.
And windows weeping and praying for me.
From the narrow window of my small cell –
I can see your big cell!

Excerpt from an Inquest

- And what do you call this country?
- My country.
- So you admit it?
- Yes, sir. I admit it.
  I'm not a professional tourist.
- Do you say 'my country'?
- I say 'my country.'
- And where is my country?
- Your country.
- And where is your country?
- My country.
- And the claps of thunder?
- My horses' neighing.
- And the gusts of wind?
- My extension.
- And the plains' fertility?
- My exertion.
- And the mountains' size?
- My pride.

- And what do you call the country?
- My country.
- And what should I call my country?
- My country . . .

There was a village called Sireen

'Palestinian village whose feudal owner
sold it for a kiss through a pane of glass . . .'

Nothing remained of Sireen after the auction,
apart from you, little prayer rug,
because a mother slyly stole you
and wrapped up her son who'd been sentenced to cold
and weaning – and later to sorrow and longing.

It's said that there was a village, a very small village,
on the border between the sun's gate and earth.
It's said that the village was twice sold –
once for a measure of oil
and once for a kiss through a pane of glass.

The buyers and sellers rejoiced at its sale,
the year the submarine was sunk,
in our twentieth century.

And in Sireen – the buyers went over the contract –
were white-washed houses, lovers, and trees,
folk poets, peasants, and children.
(But there was no school –
and neither tanks
nor prisons.)
The threshing floors, the colour of golden wine,
and the graveyard
were a vault meant for life and death,
and the vault was sold!

People say that there was a village,
but Sireen became an earthquake,
imprisoned by an amulet
as it turned into a banquet –
in which the virgins' infants
were cooked in their mothers' milk,
so soldiers and ministers
might eat along with civilization!

'And the axe is laid at the root of the tree . . .'
And once again at the root of the tree,
as one dear brother denies another
and existence. Officer of the orbits . . .
attend, O knight of death,
but don't give in –
death is behind us and also before us.
Knight of death, attend,
there is no time to retreat –
darkness crowds us and now has turned
into a rancid butter,
and the forest too is full,
the serpents of blood have slithered away
and the beaker of our ablution has been

sold to a tourist from California!
There is no time now for ablution.
People say that there was a village,
but Sireen became an earthquake,
imprisoned by an amulet
as it turned into a banquet –
in which the virgins' infants
were cooked in their mothers' milk,
so soldiers and ministers
might eat, along with civilization!

Oasis

Behind this dune we have an oasis. Leave me alone.
Leave me to rinse myself off in a bit
of its mirage. I'm tired of running after myself
to catch myself before I die.
Take – old friends and my companions – my body,
the shadow of its body's shadow,
and hold it for a while,
so I can reach my time in time.
Behind this dune we have an oasis.
Sustain your longing with dates and water,
without despair.
Listen with me to the songs of the girls
beneath the palms, but do not follow
the voice of my silence.
We have, friends, the right to die as we desire.
But there's still some hope, behind that nearby dune.

And we have the right to make the stranger
a stranger's friend,
and we have an oasis —
and a bit of rest in the house
of the loved one who left us.
He will come from behind this dune.

These poems by Samih al-Qasim are from *Sadder Than Water:
New & Selected Poems*, translated by Nazih Kassis © Ibis Editions
2006.

IBIS EDITIONS
LITERATURE OF THE LEVANT

SADDER THAN WATER:
NEW & SELECTED POEMS
SAMIH AL-QASIM

Translated from the Arabic by Nazih Kassis
Introduced by Adina Hoffman

$15.95, 965-90125-5-1, 224 pages

This selected poems by one of the leading poets in the Arab world collects work from al-Qasim's various periods and modes, and makes available to English readers for the first time ever the full range of his extraordinary oeuvre.

SARAYA, THE OGRE'S DAUGHTER
EMILE HABIBY

Translated from the Arabic by Peter Theroux

$16.95, 965-90124-5-4, 210 pages

Palestinian novelist Habiby's late masterpiece is a work of tremendous power and originality. Equal parts allegory, fairy tale, memoir, political commentary, and ode to a ruined landscape, the book is essential reading for anyone interested in the imaginative life of the Middle East.

KHIRBET KHIZEH
S. YIZHAR

Translated from the Hebrew by Nicholas de Lange and Yaacob Dweck
Afterword by David Shulman

$16.95, 978-965-90125-9-6, 136 pages

This 1949 novella about the violent expulsion of Palestinian villagers by the Israeli army has long been considered a modern Hebrew masterpiece. Yizhar's haunting, lyrical style and charged registration of the landscape are in many ways as startling as his wrenchingly honest view of one of Israel's defining moments.

www.ibiseditions.com
ibis@netvision.net.il

Croeso   Welcome

BETHLEHEM

Gyrrwch yn ofalus

Please drive carefully

Josephine Balmer
The Word for Sorrow: A Journey Ends

In the autumn of 2005, *MPT* (3.3) published the first eight
poems from my then newly-commenced work, *The Word for
Sorrow*. This aimed to intersperse versions of Ovid's often-
neglected exile poems, *Tristia*, written after his sudden and
mysterious banishment from Rome to the Black Sea in October
A.D. 8, with a series of poems exploring the history of the old
second-hand dictionary, bought at a fête in my home town in
Sussex, that I was using to translate them. As I explained in my
introduction to that extract, its original owner had inscribed his
name on the flyleaf as a school-boy in January 1900 and, as I
had discovered through a chance Google, later fought with the
Royal Gloucester Hussars in the eastern campaign at Gallipoli in
World War I.

After receiving a Wingate Foundation Scholarship to work
on the project, I have now completed it and, to bookend the
previous selection, the following extract comes from the final
section of the poem, as both Ovid's and my dictionary owner's
stories come to a close. Inevitably, in the process of writing, much
has changed, moved on, been transformed. Firstly, in order to
distinguish my character from the 'Ovid' of literary tradition, my
own construct from that of the western canon, I began instead
to use his *cognomen* or family name, Naso – the name he calls

himself in his poetry – to title my new, reclaimed versions of his poems. I also soon realised that my initial perception of *Tristia* as a work where 'the mask of classical literary artifice had crumbled away to reveal the pain of the man beneath' was naïve at best, erroneous at worse; the more I translated Ovid's verse, the more I read its scholarly studies, the more I realised that it was also full of literary in-jokes, knowing mythological references, jokes and puns – a work constantly changing register, from high tragedy to high comedy in the blink of a line. I soon saw that I needed to incorporate this new reading into my own work, adding a layer of self-deprecating irony to the melancholy as in 'Naso the Barbarian' here.

But how was this new insight to be squared with the poems I was writing about the horrors of Gallipoli? The more immersed I became in the project, the more I understood how Ovid's lightness of touch, his constant changes in register, were what was required for *The Word for Sorrow* too. For one thing the letters home and diaries of British officers I'd researched were full of the same sharp changes in tone, from terror one minute to jaunty, often inane, comments the next; making the best of it, not wanting to upset loved ones with too much reality, as 'Welcome Note' here reveals.

Following my approach with Ovid, I also decided to give my dictionary owner a new name – 'Geoffrey' – not just to preserve his anonymity but also to widen my narrative net, to include the story, the testaments, not just of one man but of many of those who fought in the campaign. As I mentioned previously, I was also keen to use the device of the dictionary and its parallel lives as a jumping-off point for other themes, other layers of narrative beyond a simple Gallipoli/Tomis equation, as more and more poems explored the relationship of text to translation or translator to language. Here, as in the earlier poems, translation and original bleed into one another so that they become indistinguishable; for instance, 'Dictionary Definitions' opens with a few lines from Ovid's longest work in exile, *Tristia* 2 and 'Naso's Last Word' quotes the final lines of his last known work of exile, *Ex Ponto* 4.16. And added to the journeys of Ovid and the British soldiers, there are now my own too, exploring the battlefields of Gallipoli as I uncover their story.

The following poems complete the story as Ovid fades into the background at Tomis, disappearing off the literary map, presumably never returning to Rome. Meanwhile Geoffrey survives, invalided out of action at Gallipoli to return home as the Gloucester Hussars are recalled, a regiment of 443 officers and men reduced to 41 (they were later sent to Palestine to join Lawrence of Arabia's cavalry campaign).

Dictionary Definitions

Construct the landscape of slaughter:
lakes, hills, forts, flesh-clogged river.
The Rhine, too, fractured, splintered,
dammed with bodies and running red
with its own blood...

My job now to distinguish **caedes** from **cruor**;
the one *carnage, slaughter, a battle massacre*
and the other simply *blood, that which flows*
from the wound. And then there's lugubria
– almost comic in English – but solemn here,
of or belonging to mourning, and in the plural,
substantive, *mourning clothes, weeds for widows.*

This shroud of Latin: **amissus. mortuus**.
The dragging, leaden cloak of language:
missing in action, presumed dead.

Welcome Note

At last there is a link, a line, a letter:

I have to admit that I've been better;
I feel like a rag, seedy from dysentery,
prescribed soup, Bovril — and champagne,
half a bottle, which had me half-drunk, dizzy.
But bread and butter was the greatest treat —
marvellous after hard biscuits and bully beef.
Still, men go to hospital and are never seen again;
it's a poisonous place, very full, not well run...

On the ship we're stacked, rotten fruit in crates,
each day the dead cleared overboard for space
to swim beside us, bandages trailed like plankton.
A lad by me, head bound, lily-pale, raved for hours,
waving his tarnished trench trowel: 'Kill the bastards!'
before swivelling round to beg a pencil from us.
We thought he wanted to scribble a last note home
but he used it for lever to ease his dressing,
gore dripping down his face in baptismal blessing.

At Alexandria they gave us clean sheets, pyjamas,
the first since landing, a lifetime ago, at Suvla.
I looked in the mirror and hardly knew myself:
an old man looking back, black hair bleached
to white. I thought of the swans by the church,
wings unfolding like ancient maps or manuscripts.
Tonight the stars were half-murmured words
sliding softly into sound after far too long.

And then one of the women sang your song.

Naso Looks to the Stars

Tell me, tell me, is she thinking of me?
Shored under these northern constellations,
I watch the Bears, both Major and Minor,
as they guide ships home to Phoenicia
or Greece – and beyond; I track the Pole Star
which climbs so high it can touch the heavens
yet never dips beneath this vast ocean –
the star which, in its course, hears all, sees all,
which knows each one of our hearts' dark secrets,
which must be looking down now on the walls
of Rome (the downfall of mocking Remus –
and mine). So search out my wife there. Tell me:
does this same soft starlight shine on her face?
Is she, too, looking up at you tonight?
Tell me, tell me, is she thinking of me?
I need to have faith in my own good faith.
The stars, fixed and fiery in this cold sky,
can't tell me more than I can tell myself.
Yes, it's *you* she is thinking of, you fool,
your name that clings for ever to her lips.
Though far from you, she loves you from afar.
My love, as troubles creep up, as you reach
to touch the cold, empty space in our bed,
is it possible that you could forget?
Night falls. Heart-break comes. Both never-ending.
Your body aches from tossing and turning.
You feel sadness? I hate to be its cause.
You do not? Yet your grief should match my own,
yearning for your lost husband, our lost home . . .
I know you *are* anguished, kind, gentle wife,
but live through this mourning, all these hardships.
Somehow there is pleasure in the pain: grief
is leavened by all our tears, is lessened.
Loyalty, love, will wash away sadness.

Among the Graves: Green Hill, Gallipoli

By a broken sign down an unmarked track,
just wide enough for horse and cart to pass,
there is a hushed grove for hollow graves.
An open-air cathedral arched by pine,
four fattened cedars as sacrificial altar,
memorial slabs lined round in pews;
a stub of stones, milk teeth, broken through
for the half-formed fighting men they sowed.
Thy Glory Shall Not Be Blotted Out
claims Tom Honey's mossed inscription.
Remembered with Honour insists Gething's.
For Wilf Barton *Thy Will be Done* –
off-the-peg words from those who never came,
pattern-book blooms – chrysanthemums, aster –
perennial guardians for bone-bare tombs;
two thousand five hundred and eighty-nine
long-broken bodies that have never been found.

Back by the gate, a lone stork takes flight,
marbled butterflies brush past – 'half-mourners' –
insistent, impatient to shed black for white.
I wish now I'd spoken out, roll-called the names,
taken one small thing, at least, home to Gloucs:
rosemary sprig to dry, daisy or phlox to press
between **calamitas.** *hurt* and *healed.* **consanatus.**

Naso Seeks Quarter

Send new orders, please. If I can't go home
then a softer place of exile, a step nearer
but far enough away from these savage foes
who count our corpses as fair plunder.
As for those who revel in the killing –
fathers sending kids for slaughter,
gods thirsting for blood-drenched altars,
sons or brothers driven by their own Furies –
they don't know it yet but they are caught here
beneath these ice-veined skies, living
under the same fallen stars as me . . .

The Fall

That winter did it still the bullets
like soft flesh?
                    The worst blizzards
on Gallipoli in decades: troops snow-balled
to stay moving, slugged down rum tots,
stood greying, ice-stiff greatcoats
like abandoned armour outside dug-outs,
warmed now by the heat of their own carcass.
For the Anzacs, it was their first fall –
so beautiful, and covering all that was not...

And when the thaw came, the dead rolled
back down the hills: men, pack-animals
and something in-between, unrecognisable

until the order arrived at last:
                                        Retreat.
We had gone through so much together
the living and the dead. We belonged
together. By now we'd rather not leave
than not leave together. We hoped
they didn't hear our footsteps as we passed . . .

5 a.m., a world pared to bone, frost-
pinched, ice-splintered: December 20th
1915, the last boots echo on impacted paths.
The future didn't exist any more, it was all
so far away. Now there was only the past . . .

Naso the Barbarian

I see a world without culture, a bleak world
full of sorrow. In this place men become wolves
with no fear of Law, justice conquered by war.
For here, now, few vestiges of Greek remain
and even these are tainted by Getic burr.
Here, I can find no one who retains Latin,
not even proper names or substantive nouns.
Yet though my voice is spent, our poet's coinage,
and my native speech bankrupt, impoverished,
I talk to myself, liquidate frozen words
for this doomed art, the currency of my verse.

And then, watching the tribesmen in the markets,
bartering for goods in their common language,
while I communicate by mime or gesture,
a thought occurs: who is the barbarian here?

Up for Auction (1919)

Another chance search reveals one last link
even if there's little to connect us
beyond this dead man's lexicon, dull ink,
we'd never have spoken the same language;
for their two grand houses, Cotswold estates,
we'd be footmen or under-kitchen maids,
the servants who go in the firing line . . .

But wars end. It was all up for auction:
unread libraries, dusty house and contents,
priceless collections sold for a pittance,
value unseen. And thrown in for good luck,
a box of school-books, discarded, surplus,
rattling down the drive on a dealer's cart
and out of sight, the long trail to Sussex.

Naso's Last Word

The vultures can stop tearing at this exile's flesh
or plot to scatter my ashes — at least, not yet.
Everything might be lost, only so much life left
(to feel, to suffer this sense of doom is enough).
For where's the use in stabbing at a dead man's chest?
I don't have strength — or space — for one more cut and thrust . . .

Lover or soldier, war hero, disgraced poet —
against all odds Geoffrey came home, Naso did not;
the player, the trickster, smiling behind the mask,
teasing out the threads of sadness, refugee's path,
this twisting, transforming journey from life to art.

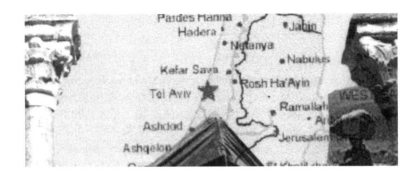

Bertil Malmberg
Five poems
Translated by Bill Coyle

Bertil Malmberg was born in Härnösand, Sweden, in 1889. He was a precocious talent, publishing five books of poetry, and a volume of translations of Schiller by the time he was thirty. From the start it was clear that he was a metrical virtuoso, though the world-weary aestheticism that characterized his early collections was not always to the critics' liking. From 1917 to 1928 Malmberg lived in Germany, where he was first fascinated, then repulsed by, the rise of fascism. He was later to publish one of the first accounts in Swedish of a concentration camp, following a visit to Dachau in 1936. His poetry, meanwhile, had deepened, growing more nuanced and self critical, and *Vinden* (*The Wind*) from 1929 contained what many consider his strongest single poem, 'Dårarna' ('The Mad'). The collection *Dikter vid gränsen* (*Poems from the Border 1935*), with its nightmarish visions of a western world in collapse, was one of the most important, and most debated, volumes of poetry published in Sweden in the 1930s and it established Malmberg as one of the major writers of his generation. In addition to his poetry, Malmberg was active as a critic, translator and dramatist, and his novel *Åkes och hans värld* (*Åke and his World*), a fictionalized account of his childhood, is a classic. In his last several collections Malmberg

made major stylistic shifts, writing primarily in free verse and
in a more concentrated, modernist style. He was inducted into
the Swedish Academy in 1953 and died in 1958. Though he
was always included in major anthologies of Swedish literature,
Malmberg's reputation went into eclipse from the 1960s on, in
spite of advocates such as the poet and novelist Lars Gustafsson.
This situation has begun to change somewhat in recent years. In
2000 the Bertil Malmberg Society (www.bertilmalmberg.org)
was founded, and a collection of his newspaper articles, *Diktaren
i sitt sekel* (*The Poet in his Century*) was published in 2006.

The Mad

I don't know what they feel, what sort of thing
they search for as they move there in a ring,

nor what it is they think when they instead
stand motionless while clouds pass overhead.

— The first one is a maharaja's son
from Nowhere Near and from Oblivion.

The second is the Baron of Chambord.
— The third is aged a thousand years or more.

The fourth is an expensive vase
of perfectly transparent glass

where now and then one might suppose
a hand beyond description sets a rose.

And each of them has his own world and space
of which no other sees a trace,

with his own lunar power and sorcery
and galaxy on galaxy.

— Far back, a few short years, the selfsame sun
lit them that shines on everyone,

and on their faces, the same sunset glowed,
and in their hourglass the same time flowed.

— Each had the same affliction — the same cry,
the same patchwork of joys as you and I.

Yes, their life was as bittersweet and prone
to imperfections as our own.

But secretly they fed a prideful dream
to salvage life from life's unceasing stream,

to build above the physical world's storm
their own dominion of perfected form.

And he who is a maharaja's son
grew furious, as at a desecration,

whenever mother would presume to speak
or pat his precious, pale-as-marble cheek.

And he who is of the nobility
languished in that small grocer's shop where he

above meal, flour and snuff caught sight
of a heraldic lily's brilliant light.

And he who's lived a thousand years and knows
how time's impoverished cloud-world goes

found dwarfish labours all too limited
and set aside his needle and his thread.

And he who is a costly vase,
a precious thing of perfectly transparent glass,

abandoned her with whom he'd been in love.
The gift she gave him was not pure enough,

and her warm words – her loving kisses – came
to seem too redolent of earth and shame.

And so they glided off till they
before long stood immensely far away.

There by a magic ring the four were bound
and the world fell to pieces all around.

– And things it seemed were out of harmony
and lacking context and affinity,

and nothing held then, and the very light
snapped like a string that had been stretched too tight . . .

They stand there now. But now the magic ring
has widened to encircle everything,

and no breeze, no disturbance can begin
to break the spell of arrogance within.

They are entirely their own code.
They are beyond the reach of bad and good.

And their attendant guardian
leads nothing but their bodies home again.

Endlessly distant, hopelessly withdrawn,
remains the maharaja's son,

remains the baron of Chambord
and he who's aged a thousand years or more,

and he who is a costly vase
of perfectly transparent glass.

– Only their bodies trudge along the way.
Around them burns the autumn day.

And their white clothing flaps around
unsteady bodies as they tramp the ground.

There is a chill, now, in the air.
October's gold leaves flutter everywhere.

The Songs of Manhood's Anguish

I
Now is the hour when you stand upon
a river bank gone misty grey
and hear how as it murmurs on
the river seems to say:

'Quick, hurry, now, my ripples small,
my foals, make haste, go on before,
and trot on bravely as I call.
I must away. I may not halt or slow.
I must away. I'm on a journey,
bound from the land Long, Long Ago
to the sea Never More.'

II
Now is the hour when you realize
how all around you dies and dies,
how the leaves' rustle at your feet
is like a prophecy and threat:
'Your destiny is clear –
all that you cherished here,
you must give back again – '
and when you look on those whom you hold dear
and, trembling, wonder, 'how much longer then?'

You walk as in a park where all around
stand trees that long have graced their ground
and lifted up their winds and might
toward heaven's unimpeded light,
trees that have known both peace and strife
and lived through most of a long life.
And frightened you can see how all around
an axe is flashing quick – now there – now here
and some archaic pine you have held dear,
its needles sparse, comes crashing to the ground.

III

And when you're seated with the people who
had built a childhood home for you
and all is still intact, although
more fragile now than years ago,
and on your cheek the spirit of that place
flickers like Christmas lights or a fire's blaze –
– yes, like a scent wherein
there lives a love that will not fail,
then suddenly the wall appears as thin
and as transparent as a veil.

And this veil can be torn away
by the first breeze's fluttering.
It has to flee. It can't delay.
It has to flee. It is a cloudlike thing.

And you with sorrow see
how this home which was your security
and its four walls,
built to keep out the weather's storms and squalls,
are insubstantial and consist
of nothing more than woven mist.

IV

And your own home you've built somehow
is no more safe or solid now
and all too often in your house there fall
black, dusky days that more resemble nights,
and, look, the prisms that have mirrored all
your careless parties' masquerades and lights –
doesn't a trembling sometimes go through these
as through the crowns of aspen trees?

When I look into myself

When I look into myself, it is always and evermore
water and cloud that I see,
something gliding and fluid and unsure
that further bewilders me.
– it is fog and glare and heavens that lour
and a sorrow no one can guess
and something that lures with rhythmic power
and seduces with endlessness . . .

I am a being of secret light

I am a being
of secret light,
who passes over
your house tonight

and casts into
your room a gleam
of the eternal
and sublime.

But before you fathom
what you see
I glide away
and cease to be.

Blinder, your heart
closes again –
and darkness on darkness
enshrouds you then.

Draw me from the room's shadow

Draw me from the room's shadow
into the ring of light,
reassure me I'm yours
and hold me tight.
I have such strange ideas
that decency requires
I hide them, such pale, unseemly,
being-less desires.

It's as if I were an outcast
from my familiar sphere.
I see with the eyes of a stranger
the things I once knew here.
If I try to speak like others,
the words come stumbling forth.
My mother tongue is rainfall
over a fogbound earth.

It's as if I were no longer
a fleshly son of man
– only a demon, uncertain,
irresponsible, wan
– as if all that I carry
were a shadowy pack of lies
– all that marks me as human
but a disguise.

It's as if I wanted not to
live in a house but take flight
and on pale wings go gliding
through the moon's snowy light,
haunting the common's leaf-fall,
ranging the fog's retreat
ungraspable and distant
and isolate.

Carlos Marzal
Four poems
Translated by Nathaniel Perry

Carlos Marzal was born in Valencia in 1961 and lives still in that city. He has published five books of poetry, most recently *Metales Pesados* (2001), which was awarded the National Critics Prize and the National Prize for Literature, and *Fuera de Mí* (2004), for which he received the Loewe Foundation Prize. His books of poetry were in 2005 collected in *El Corazón Perplejo (Poesía Reunida, 1987-2004)*, and in 2005 he published a novel, *Los Reinos de la Causalidad*. To read the recent poems of Carlos Marzal is to read the work of a fearless writer, unafraid to engage the world, and our existence in it, on its own often senseless and overwhelming terms. His is a mind bent on analyzing the human experience at face value: as a series of nearly inexplicable events, rendered almost incomprehensible by our inadequate minds. If something is beautiful, he engages that beauty directly. If something is awful, he examines our awe. The four poems here are from the most recent two collections published in Spain and exemplify, to my mind, these philosophical turns and obsessions in Marzal's newest work.

Uneasy Cathedral

High up in the vestibule
the stained glass of the arch sifts
morning's first light,
which flows, in polychrome, to the floor.

From its eminent altar,
the austere oval of a clock
prays sternly
to the god of human time
pretending that time passes,
convincing us, with its artifice, that we pass.

Our fervour finds a path in the warp
of steel, offered and occluded
by the mouth of the station platform.

I am outside time,
in a sunken time. Everything flows
and shares a pulse, commingles,
converges in the dawn:

the trail of a steam-engine floats
in motionless air; there are top hats,
columns of soldiers heading for the front;
with packs on their shoulders, tourists

pass with porters
who haul along trunks
bound for spectral European expresses.
Everything is happening always,
everything imposed on one instant.

In this uneasy cathedral,
I hear the flocking of goodbyes,
the welcomings that have come and have already gone,
and for leaving had come.
                                        Nothing succumbs.
Nothing will vanish forever.

There is but one train, one passenger.
There is one trip and one destination,

this station a tear-bottle
                                        for all pain and for gladness.

A Market in July
for Enric Sória

Out by the jetty, in the twilit air,
lazy boats recited the peaceful
soliloquy of wood rocking
and crossing water.

Content in the timeless scene,
in a wide gathering of harmonies
resolving to a surface clarity,
two half-naked boys
sat mending nets on the pier.

An indulgent salt-filled breeze
tempted us to breathe in the world
with complacent breath,
filling our lungs with only certain things.
A bloodless sun gave boathouses
the tint of foreign gold.

The dockside afternoon ended
in an apogee of vanishing light.

When we arrived at the market house,
merchants were hawking their wares.
There was an ancient echo in the tumult,
a bodily reminiscence
of all the body knows without knowing
but relives in the turning of time
—that endless lesson which pulses,
incessantly, beneath a market.

Astonished, I surveyed the stalls:
on crushed ice, austere
fish were dying. The tin-light
of their tremulous scales
made martyrdom strange.
In the motionless eyes of the fish,
we beheld a deceptive panic.
With last rasping breaths, their sad lips
curled to kiss and kissed nothing.

But in the ceremony of that summer
the strangest thing was our happiness,
the commotion which swelled in us
at the beauty of endings.
        It frightened us to enjoy the sacrifice,
to assume the fury of gods
content only with blood.

What euphoria in death when we make it.
And what satisfaction we give to inglorious death.

Away from Me

In this lightness, convalescent,
in this fragile bound skeleton,
I tell my story,
and I tell it trembling.

This hanging thread; it stitches me,
and I embark —within myself, without myself—
lifting the anchor-line
that ties my body to land and also lets me go.

Good voyage and good health—
this cliff
the current wheels around unaided,
with me here only shimmering
in a cloche of flesh.

Great winds shake my little boat, and I keep flowing.
Gales rock my little boat, and I keep being born.

Good voyage and good health—
for no one's yet returned.
From this weakness, I want something firm.
The more I allow myself, the more I enjoy myself
when I am freed, within myself, from unnecessary things.

With innocent aching, I kiss open my eyes
and calm this light fever.

These simple verses are a bonfire
in whose encircling flames I make a shelter,
and I watch wide-eyed
the constellated heavens,
and I howl down the moon,
and I articulate,
and I dance,
and I am my own tribe.

Prehistoric Place

With the most ancient of thirsts,
kneeling,
seeking the course of your waters,
I have washed myself with you,
radiant lymph;
I have lain prostrate in you,
never before so young.

In the cavern that divides your body
I have at last abandoned my own shores,
I have submerged myself in your lips
with my lips.
My saliva spoke to you without language.

With sacred humidity,
I have painted
the silken walls of your abyss.

In the brackish resin of desire,
I set down a rose,
and I have bitten it.

I set free a bird,
and I have killed it.

A man was standing here,
        and now there is nothing.

Eeva-Liisa Manner
Three poems
Translated by Emily Jeremiah

The work of Eeva-Liisa Manner (1921-1995) is little known outside her native Finland. The German translator Stefan Moster claims that were Manner better known, she would likely be counted as one of the most significant poets of European modernism. I offer here a glimpse of Manner's spare yet shimmering poetry, in the hope that it usefully tantalizes an English-speaking audience.

Manner was born in Helsinki 5 December 1921. Her mother died the following day, and Manner grew up at her grandparents' house in Viipuri, in Karelia. In 1939 the Winter War between Finland and the Soviet Union broke out. It meant that Manner, like many others, was forced to move away from the area. She went to Helsinki, where she worked first at an insurance company, then as a literary editor. In 1946, two years after the publication of her first collection of poetry, she became a freelance writer and translator. In the 1950s Manner left Helsinki to live in a village in Häme, a province in the south-west of Finland. Here, she wrote her breakthrough collection *Tämä matka* (*This Journey*, 1956). It was applauded by critics and by the public, and was enormously influential; it is now considered a landmark text of Finnish modernism.

Manner moved to Tampere in 1957, and the city remained

her place of residence until her death. She travelled frequently, however. Spain, where she first went in 1963, was particularly important to her, and she spent long periods of time in Andalusia. She also travelled to Estonia, Greece, Italy, Japan, North Africa, and Poland. She produced not only a substantial body of poetry, but also prose fiction, plays for stage and radio, reviews, essays, and translations (of Büchner and Kawabata, for example). She received numerous prizes and awards for her work. Manner did not court publicity, however, preferring solitude. Manner died in Tampere 7 July 1995.

(*Many thanks to Fleur Jeremiah, my mother, for her comments on early drafts of the translations - they were invaluable. A larger selection of translations will shortly be published by Black Sandal, whose co-founder Hilary Kassman I also thank.*)

The Town

How the houses have grown in this town,
the gulfs deepened, the water blackened;
soon it'll creep onto the streets, the railings are rickety,
the ground-water's rising, the cellars are full,
fear is rising, fear is hidden
behind oppressive discretion,
and flagrant offences.
Soon we'll need boats, d'you hear the roar,
take to the boats, hats are no use now;
or if you plunge in bravely,
carry the word beyond the distress lights.

(1956)

When shore and reflection are one
and the marriage of sky and water is intact and still,

when the mirror's fantasy is deep and clear,
and animals wander, and clouds, and the dark forest
rustles windlessly in its depths,

all that is needed to break the illusion
is a bird, dipping its wing into the water:
light and water's joyful confession to the world,
silk-thin; but it forges a union.

And the world, fresh and lovely as after rain or Creation,
or a change of mind or a long illness,
is sole, heavy, limb for limb alone.

(1960)

The world is a poem of my senses

The squares, the rushing cars, the trees, the dusty green
acquire their tone from me;
the world is a poem of my senses
and ceases when I die.
This proximity, this lengthy moment, the soft feel
of skin, are only in me, for me; an impression
or a ring around the illusion of my senses.
When I borrow from you an objective eye
I see (as through reversed binoculars)
how you walk along the bright streets,
the two of you, in the light of the awnings,
you are far away, ever further, still
you are, but small, disappearing.

(1966)

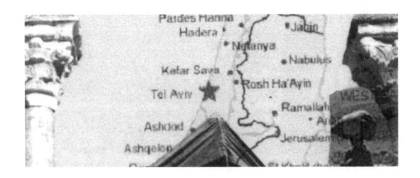

Kristiina Ehin
Six poems
Translated by Ilmar Lehtpere

Kristiina Ehin (1977) lives and works in Estonia as a freelance writer. She has an M.A. in Comparative and Estonian Folklore from Tartu University and has published four volumes of poetry in her native Estonian as well as a book of short stories. A volume of fairy tales will soon be published and a production of her play is planned for next year. Her work appears regularly in leading English language literary magazines and *The Drums of Silence*, a selection of her poems in English translation published by Oleander Press (2007), was shortlisted for the Poetry Society Popescu Prize for European Poetry in Translation. *Noorkuuhommik - New Moon Morning*, a dual language volume of her poetry, is published in Estonia by Huma (2007). Translations of her prose and her play are in preparation. She has worked as a translator, a creative dance teacher, a teller of fairy tales at a school for children with special needs and as a nature reserve warden on Mohni, an uninhabited island off the north coast of Estonia. *Kaitseala (Protected Area)*, the volume of poems she wrote there, received Estonia's most prestigious poetry prize from the Estonian Cultural Endowment. In addition to English, her poetry has been translated into ten other languages.

1

when we die we go to the land of the dead
not thinking how – we know where to go
we see behind our own eyes
    and into our hearts' tributaries

      after long long winter
      the soles of feet are tender
    like the skin on a foal's eyelids
in spring in spring – elegantly down the stairs
    and then along the cobblestones
      where it hurts a little to walk
        without shoes

      hot hot day
between the jaws of dewy morning and cool evening
    your breath wilts me parches me
      burns my northern cheeks

      birds birds
birds over rivers birds over graves
    birds over camomile and steps of stone
birds over islets and treetops birds over meadows –
            birds birds
        and their caaa-a-ll

2

I am the big drowsy queen bee
of a honeycomb universe
who sleeps alone
in her beehive-silent bed
amid the dark of winter

I feel the restless lines in the hand of this universe
I have crept through each of its black holes

when spring comes
I bring a thousand larvae into the world
drunk on my andromeda milk
they stagger out of the hive
to swing on the opening blossoms of the cosmos
to roll light's pollen
into the hot coal
of the night sky.

3

the moon throbs in the sky
peonies wait for morning and happiness
still asleep with my hands in fists
when the first sun slips over the threshold
I write myself out of the shadows
is it good so?
together with myself
in spring
yes

bolts and blinds
flutter and click shut
unexpected rain beats against the roof
metallic and reed-delicate sounds
the smell of heather
the clock ticking and heartbeats fill the time
as I bend down over eternity

I am an island
you are an island
and in the distance shines
only a shred of reality

4

outside it is rampant July
it is the lush festival of umbellifers
and stinking seaweed flirts on the stones
outside it is rampant July
and I don't want to step out into it

I want to stay in the night-time movings of dry firs
with you who walk on your hands
whisper deep friendship
breathe grey peace
into my trembling nostrils

thorns warn us
there are perilous words
suffocating belts
and poisoned apples

but there are also seagulls
in whose light there can be no doubt

listen to me
wearer of night's coats
who walks on your hands
rebellious one

august time has begun

5

drought

night
and the peppers are dropping their leaves
I cry even
when joy is too great
the wind withdraws into itself
and takes the rain along
six birds scurry off
in search of it

and again darkness falls
drought sucks the soul out of the field
and my throat already
dry as a candleflame
six birds under way
there is no wind or rain
still a little water in the cactus and the night

so already the seventh day unfurls
rain will come if you dance all night
my lips tremble
the heart of a little bird
beats against the cracked palms of my hands

Now get the gourds ready
then the wind will come
and the rain its blind brother
this night the rumble of drums has to
sway the skies
and you to whirl in the dust of drought

6

the sky drew in closer
night withdrew
cast off its dark clothes

before me stood Day
that naked man

startled I quickly got dressed

I tried to hide myself from his sharp gaze
Day
watched me as he would a bird of the night
a homeless owl that has slipped out of its nest of darkness
into the light
still unaware of its own beauty

Day
feels my ears
smooths the feathers on my back
I believe trust and fall asleep
in his heart

Dannie Abse
'Dafydd ap Gwilym at Llanbadarn'
(With a note on Dafydd by Mary-Ann Constantine and a text and a plain translation of 'The Girls of Llanbadarn' from the University of Swansea)

Dafydd ap Gwilym at Llanbadarn

I don't give a monkey-nut for their prissy talk.
Sunday – forgive me, Lord – is an amiable time
to chase the chaste. After church of course.
But no unburdened smile or sweet kiss ever
from one starched lady of Llanbadarn.
And me, so randy, I can hardly walk.

Give them boils, Lord, since none my needs assuage
– not even she whose nose seems like a chair
for spectacles! I ache. If only one, in luck,
roused me in the heather then Garwy himself
would stagger back envious and awestruck.
Lesbians they must be. Give them pox, Lord, and age.

When, parasolled, they left the church slow-paced
along the gravel pathway, past the grand
shadow of the yew, I winked, I whispered.
Nun-faced they frowned their strait-laced Never!
So I, as true a stud as Garwy stand
near graves, full of sperm. Oh what a waste!

Note on Dafydd

Dafydd ap Gwilym is probably still the Welsh-language poet best-known outside of Wales. Writing in the mid-fourteenth century, his poems brought something quite new to the already venerable Welsh poetic tradition – a speaking voice, a persona, and a wry, humorous, teasing one at that. He is maddeningly elusive in the historical record, and most of what we know about him, or think we know about him, comes from the poems themselves. He writes a great deal about his exploits and his disasters in love, about his relationship with the beautiful Morfudd and her odious husband the Bwa Bach (Little Crooked One). His language is luxuriant, both traditional (praise of fair women, of generous patrons, seductive evocations of trees and birdsong) and outrageously modern: he piles up similes and metaphors drawn from contemporary life – coinage, tools, weaponry, taxes. His technique is brilliant: light, supple and utterly self-assured. He made the *cywydd* form (rhyming couplets of seven syllables in which one rhyme is accented and the other unaccented, all shot through with clever half-rhymes and alliteration) absolutely his own.

Dafydd travelled widely, and there are traditions connecting him with many parts of Wales, but it is most likely his native patch was Brogynin, an area just outside Aberystwyth. The parish of Llanbadarn, where this poem is set, is therefore home territory for him, which may explain his lack of success with the local girls.

Text and translation from Dafydd ap Gwilym.net (University of Swansea)

Merched Llanbadarn

Plygu rhag llid yr ydwyf,
Pla ar holl ferched y plwyf!
Am na chefais, drais drawsoed,
Ohonun yr un erioed,
Na morwyn, fwyn ofynaig,
Na merch fach na gwrach na gwraig.
Pa rusiant, pa ddireidi,
Pa fethiant na fynnant fi?
Pa ddrwg i riain feinael
Yng nghoed tywylldew fy nghael?
Nid oedd gywilydd iddi
Yng ngwâl dail fy ngweled i.
   Ni bu amser na charwn –
Ni bu mor lud hud â hwn –
Anad gŵyr annwyd Garwy,
Yn y dydd ai un ai dwy,
Ac er hynny nid oedd nes
Ym gael un no'm gelynes

Ni bu Sul yn Llanbadarn
Na bewn, ac eraill a'i barn,
A'm wyneb at y ferch goeth
A'm gwegil at Dduw gwiwgoeth.
A chwedy'r hir edrychwyf
Dros fy mhlu ar draws fy mhlwyf,
Syganai y fun befrgroyw
Wrth y llall hylwyddgall, hoyw:
   'Godinabus fydd golwg –
Gwyr ei ddrem gelu ei ddrwg –
Y mab llwyd wyneb mursen
A gwallt ei chwaer ar ei ben.'
   'Ai'n rhith hynny yw ganthaw?'
Yw gair y llall geir ei llaw,

'Ateb nis caiff tra fo byd,
Wtied i ddiawl, beth ynfyd!'
    Talmithr ym rheg y loywferch,
Tâl bychan am syfrdan serch.
Rhaid oedd ym fedru peidiaw
Â'r foes hon, breuddwydion braw.
Gorau ym fyned fal gŵr
Yn feudwy, swydd anfadwr.
O dra disgwyl, dysgiad certh,
Drach 'y nghefn, drych anghyfnerth,
Neur dderyw ym, gerddrym gâr,
Bengamu heb un gymar.

The Girls of Llanbadarn

I am bent with wrath,
a plague upon all the women of this parish!
for I've never had (cruel, oppressive longing)
a single one of them,
neither a virgin (a pleasant desire)
nor a little girl nor hag nor wife.
What hindrance, what wickedness,
what failing prevents them from wanting me?
What harm could it do to a fine-browed maiden
to have me in a dark, dense wood?
It would not be shameful for her
to see me in a bed of leaves.
There was never a time when I did not love –
never was any charm so persistent –
even more than men of Garwy's ilk,
one or two in a single day,
and yet I've come no closer to winning one of these

than if she'd been my foe.
There was never a Sunday in Llanbadarn church
(and others will condemn it)
that my face was not turned towards the splendid girl
and my nape towards the resplendent, holy Lord.
And after I'd been staring long
over my feathers across my fellow parishioners,
the sweet radiant girl would hiss
to her companion, so wise, so fair:
'He has an adulterous look –
his eyes are adept at disguising his wickedness –
that pallid lad with the face of a coquette
and his sister's hair upon his head.'
'Is that what he has in mind?'
says the other girl by her side,

'While the world endures he'll get no response,
to hell with him, the imbecile!'
I was stunned by the bright girl's curse,
meagre payment for my stupefied love.
I might have to renounce
this way of life, terrifying dreams.
Indeed, I'd better become
a hermit, a calling fit for scoundrels.
Through constant staring (a sure lesson)
over my shoulder (a pitiful sight),
it has befallen me, who loves the power of verse,
to become wry-necked without a mate.

Jerzy Harasymowicz
Three poems
Translated by Maria Rewakowicz

Jerzy Harasymowicz (1933–1999) was one of the leading poets of twentieth-century Poland. His first volume *Wonders* was published in 1956. He made his debut with four other poets, Miron Białoszewski, Stanisław Czycz, Bohdan Drozdowski and Zbigniew Herbert. The arrival of this group was a milestone in twentieth-century Polish literature since it signalled a clear departure from the social-realist poetry of the day.

Harasymowicz's early books led Czeslaw Milosz, the Nobel Laureate, to write as follows about his work:

His metaphorical inventiveness seems unlimited, and he builds his tenderly or cruelly humorous stories in verse on the sensuous qualities of the simplest things he observes. I see a basic difference between such a poet as Harasymowicz and the poets of America or France: his imagination is not urban and, consequently, he can name an astonishing number of plants, trees, birds, often playing with those names and inventing images by mixing nature with the history of art. The medieval city of Krakow is often present in his poems, but the woods and remote villages of the highlands are particularly close to his heart. His stubborn clinging to poetry conceived as the realm of personal myths protects him from those who ask for 'meaning' and he has always maintained a complete indifference to ratiocinations.

Harasymowicz is not simply a poet of escapist imagination and fancy. His provocative vision helps reinvent his readers' ability to experience and deeply feel reality. In his poetry, tradition and the past are juxtaposed with contemporary, everyday reality. This irony is often rendered with warm humour which suffuses much of his poetry with fantastic and comic wit.

His cultural roots which encompassed Polish, Ukrainian and German backgrounds, afforded him a sensitivity to national difference – and struggle. To declare his wide allegiances as a poet at the meeting point of past, present, and East European identities, he requested that his ashes be scattered at a mountain pass in the Beskyd Mountains where a plaque now memorializes his acts of affirmation.

Contemporary poets speak of their spiritual connection with Harasymowicz who remains to this day a unique and highly original presence in Polish literature.

She Tells Me

She is charming
but the more
she recalls the joyous groves
of her past

while at the same time
her arms and legs
fight me off
like a rapacious
hawthorn bush

the less I know
if her heart
is a tent
in which I shall dwell

My pride
is badly wounded
I saddle my horse
for departure

Wiersze milosne, 1979 (Love Poems)

My Friend's House

Long rafts of lowlands
Drift by
With my friend's house
On one of them

God sits up in the rye-field
Like a rabbit
The Madonna's bosom grows quietly
Like a loaf of bread

Mother drags
A widow's veil across the field-patch
Her palms are run through
With streaks of kindness

A green flame flickers
In the lowland's window
A cow entreats heavens
For long troughs

From afar
Nightingales peck my heart
But I prefer pigs'
good-natured grunts

As always
The dead appear
Like fish in the river
Around dusk

In my friend's yard
The grass is so thick
That one needs
A currycomb to comb it

It's good to lie down on one's back
And to fall asleep
The night will walk around the orchard
With a white cane

From a cellar's mound
Christ will rise
And walk
Drunken through the village

Like a quail
His overcoat will trail across the wheat-field
And grow
Under my friend's pen

Polska weranda, 1973 (The Polish Porch)

The Kitchen

Leaves fly
onions fly
the kettle's landscapes sing
the kitchen fills with a fog of emotions

The kettle
sits on my mother's shoulder
like a falcon

A cathedral of blue pots
rises
in autumn rain
an old steamboat sways
on the ironing board

And everything's covered with thick vapours
and a sugar-bowl rings incessantly

For others – there is Greece where columns
and heroes' helmets grow

For me – the kitchen
where reality crumbles
in a saucepan

For me – the deep-water flora
of barley soups
red corals
of borsch

For me – the kitchen's tropics
exotica of huge baobabs of dill
ever higher pagodas of plates

Gobelins of oilcloths
with golden flowers of broth
big-headed icons
of dark ladles

For me – playing on a curved stick of rhubarb
writing kitchen poems

Polska weranda, 1973 (The Polish Porch)

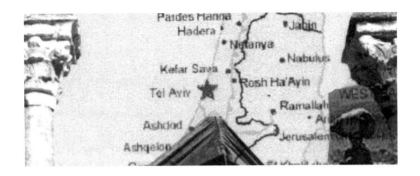

Reviews

Ted Hughes
Selected Translations
edited by Daniel Weissbort
Faber and Faber
232 pp £20.00 ISBN 0-571-22140-8

With *MPT* now in its third series, it seems fitting to review
a text by its two co-founders. Daniel Weissbort provides both
an insider's knowledge of Hughes' working practices and a
retrospective on why they started *MPT* in the first place—a
decision triggered by Hughes' encounter with various East
European poets in the fifties and linked to his role in establishing
the annual Poetry International festival n London. The result
is a substantial, academic text that includes an introduction
to Hughes' translation theory; separate introductions to each
poet; previously unpublished translations; appendices of letters,
collaborators' prose cribs and editors' commentaries from the first
edition of *MPT*—a vast array of 'behind the scenes' material and
insights which make this an essential text for poetry translators,
students of translation theory and Hughes specialists.

Hughes' interest in translation was driven partly by idealism,
and partly by his own needs as a poet, not to mention the fact
that he was in great demand as translator for the theatre. The
Weissbort/Hughes collaboration reflected a desire for 'global

unity'; as Hughes explains in his programme note to Poetry International '67, poetry was the means whereby various nations could 'make a working synthesis of their ferocious contradictions'. One can sense his passionate engagement with poets such as the Hungarian János Pilinszy and the Israeli Yehudai Amichai, who only came to people's attention in the West by being showcased in *MPT*. This idealism triggered his interest in the possibilities of a universal language that culminated in his collaboration with Peter Brook to perform *Orghast*, a short dramatic piece consisting entirely of made-up words. Indeed, passion is the driving force of all Hughes' translations, produced almost always from poems that resonate with his own—that can 'be of use' to him. Take for example 'The Boy Changed into a Stag Cries Out at the Gate of Secrets' by the Hungarian Ferenc Juhász, which chimes with Hughes' interest in the violence inherent in nature:

> The mother called after her son
> from the far distance
> she went out in front of the house, calling
> and she loosened her hair's thick knot
> which the dusk wove to a dense, stirring veil,
> a valuable robe sweeping the earth,
> wove to a stiff and heavily flaring mantle,
> a banner for the wind with ten black tassels,
> a shroud, the fire-slashed blood-heavy twilight.

Of course, given his interest in myth, Hughes was most likely to find rich pickings in classical texts: Homer, Seneca, Ovid, Aeschylus and Euripides. Reading the extracts both from the above writers, as well as from Lorca's *Blood Wedding* and Racine's *Phèdre*, all conveying the natural, clear and economic language that sounds so powerful on stage, one can understand why Hughes would have received so many theatre commissions.

When working with contemporary poets he relied on personal communication and literal cribs. In the case of classical texts he often drew on previous editions (usefully cited by Weissbort), but the literal crib was his preferred option, enabling him to get close to the original. This focus on the 'literal' was another passion for Hughes and Weissbort:

> We feel that as soon as devices extraneous to the original are employed for the purpose of recreating its 'spirit', the value of the whole enterprise is called into question.
>
> (*MPT* No. 1, 1965)

We can be grateful for Hughes' belief in the literal since it means he steers clear of formal metres and rhyme, so often the downfall of many translators of pre-twentieth texts in particular. Yet it also suggests either a surprising obliviousness to the complexities of language or an underplaying of his own talents. For there can never be a single 'literal' translation; translators have always to make numerous choices with regard to diction, structure, syntax etc. With Hughes it seems to be a case of 'do as I do rather than do as I say' and one can learn a lot by looking at what he actually does in his 'literal' translations. He avoids formal metre and rhyme and omits as much as possible, streamlining the translation. He uses strong diction that sounds like his own voice, allowing monosyllabic words to dominate, and gives the language cohesion through repetition, alliteration and a whole range of other patternings. In places he also uses unrhymed trimeter, creating a fairly regular beat though with some variation. Yet like all good craft the end result gives the illusion of being easy.

What he produces is poetry attuned to the modern ear. Thus with the dramatic verse we have characters who sound like real people. The self-loathing of Phèdre here is totally convincing:

Oh God, what am I doing? What am I saying?
I think I'm losing my senses.
Me jealous? Me beg Theseus
To avenge my jealousy? Implore my husband
To remove my rival
From my monstrous passion for his son?

A good example of this complex approach in his supposed 'literal'
versions is in this rendering of Ovid's *Metamorphoses*:

. . . Pierced by the mortal beauty of Adonis
She has forgotten Cythera's flowery island,

Forgotten the bright beaches of Paphos,
Forgotten Cnidos, delicate as its fish,
Amathus, veined with costly metals. Neglected

Even Olympus. She abstains from heaven
Besotted by the body of Adonis.
Wherever he goes, clinging to him she goes.

Various techniques are used to give the verse cohesion: alliteration
(of the kind Hughes admires in middle English) such as 'besotted
by the body', along with the repetitions of 'forgotten' or 'goes'.
He also uses the list of settings – 'Cythera', 'Pathos', 'Cnidos' – to
build to a climax with 'Olympus'.

It is particularly pleasing to see Hughes providing us with
evidence that Pushkin, so rarely translated well (because of some
establishment rule that his musical metres must be retained
in translation), can be successfully rendered via the Hughesian
ideology. Here we have Pushkin's 'The Prophet', powerfully
rendered with not a rhyme in sight, just strong use of the simple
past followed by a shift to the imperative and a not too obvious
unrhymed trimeter:

He split my chest with a blade,
Wrenched my heart from its hiding,
And into the open wound
Dropped a flaming coal.
I lay on stones like a corpse.
There God's voice came to me:
'Stand, Prophet, you are my will.
Be my witness. Go
Through all seas and lands. With the Word
Burn the hearts of the people.'

The single flaw in this otherwise excellent book lies in its lay-
out. Weissbort, in a keenness to present Hughes's translations
chronologically, does not differentiate between drafts and
finished works. The presentation of the translations themselves
might have been better served by keeping archive versions that
are clearly not polished poems as part of another appendix. This
aside, Weissbort has provided a real *tour de force* for all who
admire Hughes.

Belinda Cooke

Shorter Reviews

Taha Muhammad Ali, *So What: New & Selected Poems 1971-2005*, translated by Peter Cole, Yahya Hijazi & Gabriel Levin, Bloodaxe Books, 224pp, paperback, £12, ISBN: 978-1-85224-792-8/

Mahmoud Darwish, *The Butterfly's Burden*, translated by Fady Joudah, Bloodaxe Books, 344pp, paperback, £12, ISBN: 978-1-85224-788-1 (both bilingual Arabic-English editions)

Two essential new editions of Palestinian poetry. Cole's versions, written in collaboration with Hijazi & Levin, capture Muhammad Ali's sparse, poignant verse and semi-colloquial yet unflinching voice, reminding us, as Cole notes in his introduction, that 'the conflict in Israel-Palestine involves not merely a clash of ideologies...but, above all, a struggle to preserve an essential dignity'. As Muhammad Ali writes of his eponymous protagonist in 'Abd el-Hadi Fights a Superpower': 'His God-given rights are a grain of salt/tossed into the sea.' And yet 'were he to encounter/ the entire crew/ of the aircraft carrier *Enterprise*/he'd serve them eggs/sunny-side up/and labneh/fresh from the bag'.

Mahmoud Darwish's poetry is already familiar to readers of *Modern Poetry in Translation* with an extract from his extraordinary 2003 work, *A State of Siege* appearing in MPT 3.1 (translated by Sarah Maguire) and new versions of his work by Fady Joudah and John Berger published in this issue. Bloodaxe's new selection, again translated by Joudah, includes another long extract from *A State of Siege* as well as from his 1998 collection of love poetry, *The Stranger's Bed* and his recent 2003 collection of lyrics, *Don't Apologise for What You've Done*. American-Palestinian poet Joudah's translations are, as ever, worthy of their source material – sensual, discursive, urgent: 'I palpate you as a violin palpates the silk of the faraway time/and around me and you sprouts the grass of an ancient place – anew'.

Amir Or, *Day*, translated from the Hebrew by the author and
Fiona Sampson, Dedalus, 83pp, £8.20, ISBN: 1-904556-52-3

'Language is a wound,' notes Hebrew poet Amir Or in his
poem 'Language Says', 'from which the world flows and flows.'
Day, the second section of a trilogy begun with *Poem* (published
by Dedalus in 2004), offers a series of poems centred around the
Jewish Book of Prayers, translated with exemplary precision by
Fiona Sampson. As John F. Deane points out in his afterword
to the volume, for Or, language is 'more than a method of
communication . . . it is a power in itself'. Or's resulting poetry
is dense and spiritual, yet still colloquial, equally concerned
with the everyday life of 'the salary raise falsely promised,/the
grandson's bar-mitzvah, a memory of perfume from last night', as
well as 'the news/that the Number 5 bus was blown up . . . before
I woke up.' An expert on ancient Greek philosophy and religion,
and a national coordinator of the UN-sponsored 'Poets for Peace',
Or writes of a world torn apart by violence where still the 'heart
is yearning but not afraid'.

Gennady Aygi, *Field-Russia*, translated by Peter France, New
Directions, 144pp, paperback, $15.95, ISBN: 978-0-8112-1721-7

Shortly before Russian poet Gennady Aygi's untimely death
from cancer in 2006, he arranged this selection of poems with his
long-term translator and friend Peter France, to be collected from
Aygi's previous 'lyric-books' and to constitute what he considered
his 'life-book'. Nominated several times for the Nobel Prize,
Aygi's verse both harks back to a mystical rural paganism as well
as looking forward to the post-modern age – a mysteriousness
and profundity that France's versions capture with grace: 'in
the field towards matins-the-sun,' as 'Field: Unknown Flower'
directs, 'with light-of-beauty/as with speech/of wisdom/shining'.
(See Peter France's tribute to Aygi in *MPT* 3/6.)

Guy Goffette, *Charlestown Blues: Selected Poems*, edited and translated by Marilyn Hacker, University Of Chicago Press, 160pp, hardback, £15, ISBN: 0-226-30074-9 (bilingual French-English edition)

Lauded French poet and translator Guy Goffette's lyrical, urbane verse is the natural heir to that of Verlaine and Rimbaud. In this first English edition of his work, the equally distinguished American poet and translator, Marilyn Hacker, captures the wit and musicality of Goffette's French: 'And the caesura which parks itself right in the middle/like a guy in overalls in a bathroom full/of mermaids. There we go, the sea again/ – but how can I say I love you/ without stumbling into its snares?' Marvellous.

Jane Tozer, *Knights of Love: after The Lais of Marie de France*, Fal Publications, 280pp, paperback, £12, ISBN: 978-0-95449-808-5.

Jane Tozer's versions of Marie de France come garlanded with much-deserved awards in both the John Dryden and the Times/Stephen Spender Poetry in Translation prizes. Now available in a lovely edition by Cornish publisher Fal, this is a wonderfully warm and witty read for anyone interested in French literature, in poetry and, of course, in love. Tozer is a master of rhyme and has an ear for a pithy phrase which keeps the momentum moving admirably throughout: 'Despite her frantic tears and pleading/ She is disposed as stock for breeding./Her youth and beauty are degraded/Her precious innocence traded/To one whose appetites are jaded'.

Claude Vigée, *Songs of Absence*, translated by Anthony Rudolf, Menard, 55pp, paperback, £6, ISBN: 978-1-874320-59-3 (bilingual French-English edition)

Songs of Absence is a moving tribute from the distinguished French poet to Evelyne, his wife of sixty years who died in January 2007. Poignant poems translated with great delicacy by Tony Rudolf : 'Despite my turmoil, I, abandoned child,/keep her place at breakfast every morning;/before me, at the table, in the muted light,/stands a chair against the wall, still, empty, there'.

Gordon Wallace, *Fragrances of Old Cathay: Distilled from the Writings of Leading Poets of Imperial China*, Jon Carpenter, 81pp, paperback, £6.99, ISBN: 9-780954-972790

Like Jane Tozer, Gordon Wallace is another Times/Stephen Spender prize-winner (for a version of Dante *Inferno* V). A former diplomat, Wallace here collects 130 poems from imperial China, translated with elegant concision yet clarity. As he renders Li Bai's 'Song by Lake Qiu': 'The waters mirror snow that's there/ but mirrors leave me wondering where/I've gained the hoar-frost in my hair'.

Mehmet Yashin, *Wartime*, translated by Taner Baybars, The Happy Dragons' Press, 2pp, paperback, £2.20

A lovely single poem edition of Yashin's Turkish verse which explores the difficulties and dangers of speaking one's mother-tongue, hand-set and printed by letterpress with a colour lino-cut illustration by John R. Smith. The Happy Dragons is a proudly low-tech operation and so this and its other beautiful limited edition titles are available to order only from bookshops or direct from the publishers at 8, Stambourne Road, Toppesfield, Nr Halstead, Essex, CO9 4DG (send a cheque made payable to J Stafford-Baker plus 60p postage per order).

Anvil Round-Up

After the recent decision by the Arts Council to cut Anvil's funding (since reprieved), it seems timely to take a look at some of their recent titles. Always beautifully produced, with a list including the best of contemporary and classical poetry and translation, their books are a delight.

Odysseus Elytis, *Selected Poems: 1940-1979*, 160pp, paperback £9.95, ISBN: 978-0-85646-355-6

Chosen and introduced by leading translators of modern Greek poetry, Edmund Keeley and the late Philip Sherrard, with contributions from George Savidis, Nanos Valoritis and John Stathatos, this is a lovely edition of Nobel Prize Winner Elytis' poetry.

Oktay Rifat, *Poems*, translated by Ruth Christie & Richard McKane, 256pp, paperback, £11.95, ISBN: 978-0-85646-370-9

A wonderful selection of the intensely private Turkish poet's work, translated by two renowned translators. Poetry to ponder, with Rifat, 'how good to be alive/how good the world!' Essential.

Statius, *Silvae: A Selection*, versions by Anthony Howell & Bill Shepherd, 96pp, paperback, £7.95, ISBN: 978-0-85646-387-7

Much admired by past poets but now undeservedly overlooked by the classical canon, Statius' mannered yet ingenious poetry is ripe for a reappraisal. He has two excellent advocates in Howell and Shepherd who provide enthusiastic and witty new versions: 'We can't count on decent weather, dears,' as Howell's 'A Day at the Circus' opens, but nevertheless these poems provide entertainment for all.

Eliot Weinberger (ed), *The New Directions Anthology of Classical Chinese Poetry*, 272pp, paperback, £12.95, ISBN: 978-0-85646-396-9

David Hinton (ed & trans), *Mountain Home: The wilderness poetry of ancient China*, paperback, 320pp, £12.95, ISBN: 978-0-85646-395-2

Bei Dao, *midnight's gate: essays*, translated by Matthew Fryslie, paperback, 272pp, paperback, £10.95, ISBN: 978-0-85646-394-5

In two exhaustive anthologies, Anvil provide an overview of classical Chinese poetry – and its translation. Eliot Weinberger's volume collects together now-iconic versions by Ezra Pound and William Carlos Williams, alongside those by American poets Kenneth Rexroth, Gary Snyder and David Hinton. Hinton's own companion volume, *Mountain Home*, concentrates on the Chinese tradition of river-and-mountains poetry from the 5th to 13th centuries A.D – a beautiful, soothing collection: 'A slight rain comes, bathed in dawn light,' as he translates Tu Fu's 'Morning Rain', 'I hear it among treetop leaves before the mist/arrives'. In contrast, *midnight's gate* is a selection of prose writings from leading contemporary Chinese poet, Bei Dao, a travelogue charting the many cities he has lived in and visited since his exile from China in 1989, including New York, Paris, Prague and Durham where 'the streets were empty, the sky immense, and the clouds pale'. Translated by Matthew Fryslie, this is a charming and life-affirming account of what it feels like, as Dao explains, to be one of the 'barbarians at opposite borders of language'.

Josephine Balmer

Acknowledgements

Every issue of *MPT* is a collaborative endeavour of many people, but in editing *Palestine* we have had help, advice and practical kindness in extraordinary measure. We are especially grateful to the following:

Heinz Bachmann and Isolde Moser, for permission to translate and publish two letters by Jack Hamesh;

Peter Cole, Ibis Editions, for permission to reprint poems by Samih al-Qassim;

Simon Constantine, for much technical help;

Jennie Feldman, for putting us in touch with many good writers;

David Parsons, for his photograph of Bethlehem and help with place-names;

Joe Sacco, for very generously allowing us to reproduce two pages of his *Palestine* (Jonathan Cape, 2003).

Notes on Contributors

Dannie Abse's most recent publication is *The Presence* (Hutchinson, 2007)

Josephine Balmer's collections include *Sappho: Poems and Fragments, Classical Women Poets, Catullus: Poems of Love and Hate* and *Chasing Catullus: Poems, Translations and Transgressions* (all Bloodaxe). She is Reviews Editor of *Modern Poetry in Translation*, a judge for The Times/Stephen Spender Prize for Poetry in Translation and Royal Literary Fund Writing 2007/8 Writing Fellow at the University of Sussex.

John Berger: Storyteller, essayist, poet, screenwriter, dramatist. Lives in the French Alps. Most recent book: *Hold Everything Dear. Dispatches on Survival and Resistance* (Verso, London, 2007). Has also collaborated in translating Aimé Césaire and Bertolt Brecht.

Belinda Cooke's poetry, reviews and Russian translations have been published widely. She is currently completing an edition of *The Selected Writings of Marina Tsvetaeva*. She lives in Aberdeenshire.

Bill Coyle's poems and translations have appeared in journals including the *Hudson Review, PN Review* and *Poetry*. His first book of poetry, *The God of This World to His Prophet*, won the New Criterion Poetry Prize in 2006. Mr. Coyle teaches at Salem State College in Salem, Massachusetts.

Vivian Eden's latest prose translations are *Lords of the Land* by Akiva Eldar, *Idit Zertal* (Nation Books), a critical study of the Israeli settlements in the West, and Aaron Megged's seriocomic novel *The Flying Camel and the Golden Hump* (Toby Press), of which the protagonist is a literary translator.

Jennie Feldman's first collection *The Lost Notebook* (Anvil, 2006) was shortlisted for the Glen Dimplex Poetry Award. Her translations of the French poet Jacques Réda, *Treading Lightly: Selected Poems 1961-1975*, were also published by Anvil in 2006. A former award-winning radio producer and presenter, she lives in Jerusalem.

Marilyn Hacker is the author of eleven books of poetry, most recently *Essays on Departure: New and Selected Poems* (Carcanet, 2006). Her translations from the French include Guy Goffette's *Charlestown Blues* (University of Chicago Press, 2007) and Vénus Khoury-Ghata's *Nettles* (Graywolf Press, 2008). She lives in New York and Paris.

Rema Hammami is an anthropologist. Born in Saudi Arabia, she lives in East Jerusalem and teaches at the Women's Studies Institute at Birzeit University. Her recent writing has focused on the Palestinian everyday experience of Israeli military checkpoints. She and John Berger have collaborated on a number of projects in and about Palestine.

Alan Hart, born in Aberystwyth in 1951, studied German. He has written poetry since he was nine. Spent a quarter-century working overseas (half of it in Japan) and has not published recently, though always writing and sometimes translating. He teaches Communication at Queen Mary University of London.

Jonathan Holmes is a writer and theatre director. His testimony play *Fallujah* was performed in London, Berlin and Prague in 2007. In 2005 his work on John Donne led to the first performance in 400 years of several Donne songs at St. Paul's Cathedral; they are analysed in his book *Refiguring Mimesis*. He is currently collaborating with The Sixteen on a sequence of concerts combining poetry and music at the South Bank Centre, and is shooting a documentary feature entitled *Perpetual Peace*.

Emily Jeremiah is a Leverhulme Early Career Fellow in German at Royal Holloway, University of London. She is working on a book about migration and narration in contemporary women's writing.

Fady Joudah is a Palestinian-American. He is the translator of Mahmoud Darwish's most recent poetry collected in *The Butterfly's Burden* (Bloodaxe). His first book of poetry, *The Earth in the Attic* has received the Yale Series for Younger Poets Prize in 2007. He is currently working on a translation collection of Ghassan Zaqtan's recent poetry.

Nazih Kassis is a lexicographer and translator of contemporary Arabic prose and poetry. He received his doctorate in linguistics from the University of Exeter and has compiled, edited, and translated several dictionaries. A poet in the local dialect, he has taught English and Arabic at the University of Haifa and Portland State University.

Ilmar Lehtpere's translation of *The Drums of Silence*, a selection of Kristiina Ehin's poetry, published by Oleander Press, was shortlisted for the Poetry Society Popescu Prize for European Poetry in Translation. A dual language volume of his translations of Kristiina Ehin's poetry is published in Estonia by Huma. He is currently working on more of Kristiina's poetry, as well as her prose and play.

Gabriel Levin's new collection of poems, *The Maltese Dreambook*, is due out with Anvil this May. He lives in Jerusalem.

Tal Nitzan is poet, editor and one of the pre-eminent translators from Spanish in Israel. Won, among others, the Culture Minister's Prize for Translators (1995, 2005), for Beginning Poets (2001) and for First Book (2002), and ACUM (artists' rights society) Poetry Prize (2007). An ardent peace activist, Nitzan edited the ground-breaking anthology *With an Iron Pen: Hebrew Protest Poetry 1984–2004*.

Nathaniel Perry is an American poet and translator whose work has most recently appeared or is forthcoming in *American Poetry Review, West Branch, Poetry International, Water~Stone, Salamander, 32 Poems* and elsewhere. He is the editor of *lyric* and lives with his wife and two dogs in Bloomington, Indiana.

Maria G. Rewakowicz, poet, translator and literary scholar, holds a Ph.D in Slavic Languages and Literatures from the University of Toronto. Currently she is a visiting lecturer in the Dept. of Slavic Languages and Literatures at the University of Washington in Seattle.

Joe Sacco's *Palestine*, with an introduction by Edward Saïd, was published by Jonathan Cape in 2003. He is currently working on *Footnotes in Gaza*, about the southern Gaza Strip, to be published by Metropolitan Books.

Deema K. Shehabi is a Palestinian poet who grew up in the Arab world. Her poems have appeared widely in anthologies and journals such as *The Kenyon Review, Drunken Boat,* and *The Poetry of Arab Women.* She has been nominated for a Pushcart Prize, and her poems have been translated into Arabic, French, and Farsi. She is currently Vice-President of RAWI (Radius of Arab-American Writers).

Linda Stern Zisquit has published three collections of poetry, most recently *The Face in the Window,* as well as translations from Hebrew, including *Wild Light,* for which she received an NEA Grant, and *Let the Words: Selected Poems of Yona Wallach.* She lives in Israel, teaches at Bar Ilan University, and runs an art gallery in Jerusalem.

MODERN POETRY IN TRANSLATION   Series 3   Number 7

LOVE AND WAR

Edited by David and Helen Constantine

Cover by Lucy Wilkinson

Contents
Editorial   David and Helen Constantine

Price £11
   Available from www.mptmagazine.com

GETTING IT ACROSS

Edited by David and Helen Constantine

Cover by Lucy Wilkinson

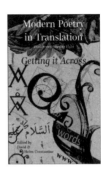

Contents
Editorial   David and Helen Constantine

Robert Walser, twelve poems, translated by Michael Hamburger
Two Memorial Notes on Michael Hamburger by Anthony Rudolf and Iain Galbraith

Reviews
Charlie Louth on Don Paterson, Martyn Crucefix and Rilke
Belinda Cooke on *The Translator as Writer* (edited by Susan Bassnett and Peter Bush)
Jo Balmer, Shorter Reviews

Price £11
   Available from www.mptmagazine.com

MPT Subscription Form

Name	Address
Phone	Postcode
E-mail	Country

I would like to subscribe to *Modern Poetry in Translation* (please tick relevant box):

Subscription Rates (including postage by surface mail)

	UK	Overseas
❑ One year subscription (2 issues)	£22	£26 / US$ 52
❑ Two year subscription (4 issues) with discount	£40	£48 / US$ 96

Student Discount*

❑ One year subscription (2 issues)	£16	£20 / US$ 40
❑ Two year subscription (4 issues)	£28	£36 / US$ 72

Please indicate which year you expect to complete your studies 20 . . .

Standing Order Discount (only available to UK subscribers)

❑ Annual subscription (2 issues)	£20
❑ Student rate for annual subscription (2 issues)*	£14

Payment Method (please tick appropriate box)

❑ **Cheque:** please make cheques payable to: *Modern Poetry in Translation.*
Sterling, US Dollar and Euro cheques accepted.

❑ **Standing Order:** please complete the standing order request below, indicating
the date you would like your first payment to be taken. This should be at least one
month after you return this form. We will set this up directly with your bank.
Subsequent annual payments will be taken on the same date each year. For UK only.

Bank Name	Account Name
Branch Address	❑ Please notify my bank
	Please take my first payment on
Post Code	......./......./......... and future payments on
Sort Code	the same date each year.
Account Number	Signature:
	Date........./........./............

Bank Use Only: In favour of Modern Poetry in Translation, Lloyds TSB,
1 High St, Carfax, Oxford, OX1 4AA, UK a/c 03115155 Sort-code 30-96-35

Please return this form to: The Administrator, Modern Poetry in Translation, The Queen's
College, Oxford, OX1 4AW   administrator@mptmagazine/www.mptmagazine.com